For Eva,

dear friend and sister,
your sister from 1/2 way across
the globe write - - - -
with love
Bindu
5/2/99. Chicago

Indelible Imprints

INDELIBLE IMPRINTS

∎

Daughters Write on Fathers

Edited by Priti T. Desai, Neela D'Souza
and Sonal Shukla

Foreword by
Neera Desai

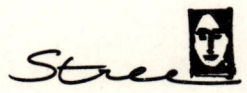

INDELIBLE IMPRINTS
Daughters Write on Fathers
was first published in January 1999 by Stree
16 Southern Avenue, Calcutta 700 026

© 1999 by Priti T. Desai, Neela D'Souza and Sonal Shukla

ISBN 81-85604-25-8

All rights reserved. No part of this book may be reproduced or utilized in any form or by any means without prior permission from the publisher

Distributed by Bhatkal Books International
Mumbai, Calcutta, Delhi, Pune

Typesetting and design by
LOGS, 6 Ram Hari Mistry Lane, Calcutta 700 013
and printed by Webimpressions (India) Pvt Ltd
34/2 Beadon St, Calcutta 700 006

Published by Mandira Sen for STREE, an imprint of
Bhatkal and Sen, 16 Southern Ave, Cacutta 700 026

To daughters everywhere

Acknowledgements

The editors thank all those who participated in this exercise, even if some contributions do not appear here. Their enthusiasm and insights were heartening and informative and kept us going during the long months that we worked on this collection. We thank Dr. Neera Desai for writing the foreword. We owe thanks too to Sandrella Joseph of Vacha for typing the first draft.

Foreword

It gives me great pleasure to welcome *Indelible Imprints.* The editors deserve congratulations for putting together such an unusual book where women have talked about their innermost feelings and perceptions about their fathers. We all know how significant personal relationships are to us; we need to appreciate their enigmatic nature to understand our lives. For some time now feminist discourse has been quite concerned about the mother's role, particularly in the lives of her daughters. Quite often, it has been found that the mother has been the mediator or the buffer between the authoritarian father and the children, especially the daughters. Since the lives of mothers and daughters are so intertwined, I wondered why the contributors have chosen to write about their fathers instead.

The prevalent norms in a patriarchal family project the father as a figure of authority and indicate a relationship where social distance between father and children, particularly daughters, has to be maintained. In our society, the daughter is seen as a transient member of the family and the inevitability of her departure from the natal family is deeply entrenched in folklore. In the context of the basic asymmetry between male and female children, the perception of the father's role from the daughter's point of view raises serious interest in women's studies and in feminist writings. Through these studies, not only do we gain an insider's view of the working of patriarchy but also of the insidious nature of its site: the family itself. The daughter even when aware of the workings of patriarchy is drawn to her father and her family by ties of affection, of what appears to be immutable precedence, of the 'naturalness' of it all. When the relationship with the father has been close and fulfilling, it has made it harder for the daughter to decipher her acquiescence. When it has been unhappy, fraught, wounding, the contributors have let us glimpse its workings.

When we look back at the initial concerns in women's studies, we are struck by the limited amount of knowledge available on women. The early explorations were confined to the depiction of the status of women, and their role, in the economy, polity, the family, in education, and so on. It was a time of making women visible. This exercise not only exposed the distorted representation of women in various academic disciplines, but also highlighted the contribution made by women in many fields. The impact of various state policies, particularly of development, on women, from women's perspectives raised certain fundamental questions regarding the status of women in society. Questioning the extant practices and norms resulted in critiquing various social science disciplines. Mainstream premises, methodologies, all began to be questioned. The realization that it was imperative to introduce gender as an analytical category to understand society began to gain ground.

The new perspective revealed the extent of the violence against women within the domestic sphere and in the wider society. New forms of sexual oppression, complex structures of dominance and serious implications of fundamentalism and communalism called for more intense focusing on women's issues. Women began to see the connections between the oppression centred in the greater society and that which was found at home, within the family, within relationships. Women were not always victims. Their resilience on the domestic front was unexpected and inspiring. Women who talked to each other, especially those who had access to women's groups, those who had joined the women's movement, talked about the question of identity, of resistance to oppression, of trying to strengthen their personalities, of giving support to their children. Aside from strengthening themselves silently, women were shaping the life of the future generation invisibly. Women's studies which had started looking at society at large, began to examine the inner stirrings, battles, the lives of women themselves.

Autobiographical writings attracted the attention of scholars as well as of activists. When we look at women's diaries and letters of the late nineteenth and early twentieth centuries, we see not just how skilled the women were as writers but also their inner feelings and perceptions about family relationships. Outwardly the women may have been silent and uncomplaining. The writings reveal otherwise. Autobiographical writing is a self-assertive act. It assumes some significance in the experiences related, entails self-searching, self-analysis, self-awareness. In a society where cultural norms expect a woman to be modest, self-effacing, docile, autobiographical writings may not provide a transparent critique. Where the normative structure expects a woman to hide her identity, writing is an act of courage. The selection of events, subjective appraisals of situations, exposing what is personal in the public area are some of the formidable hurdles that have to be faced. It is these very hurdles that the contributors and the editors of this book have negotiated: they are letting us into their private worlds—the relationships with their fathers.

Writing about families is not easy for women. They are taking on one of the strongest institutions in Indian society. The earlier assumption that a family is a homogeneous group or that all its members derive equal benefits or possess the same power and authority has been seriously questioned today. It has become clear that the family is a complex mix of dominance and nurturance, of conflict and of support. A woman's life is almost wholly lived in the family. It is the site where her psyche is constructed, and in patriarchal society a daughter's socialization has overtones of gendered structures, where ideas, norms, customs and values governing entitlements to resources are discriminatory and promote inequality. The family is on the one hand a site where girls grow up in a gendered environment; on the other hand it provides emotional support and security in the overall calculating, contractual social relationship. As some eminent social scientists have pointed out, intra-familial power structures are partly harsh and partly loving, partly conflictual and partly consensual. This contradictory feature of family relationships has always been a challenge to women and has been acutely delineated by the contributors.

Anyone who reads the book will find telling examples of authority and affection, of control and nurturance. The accounts describe the gradual breaking down of the boundary of social distance between father and daughter with the growth of education and urbanization. A reader is bound to feel that she is reading her own story. During the last four or five decades, there have been dramatic changes in educated, urban, middle class families. A daughter's education is considered not merely as a status-providing attainment for the family, but also as a gateway to tangible and non-tangible entitlements. Girls are not just educated, but are given quality education. They are encouraged to study and when they outshine their brothers, the family reacts with pride, not unmixed with disappointment at the poor results of the boys. Quite often, girls out-perform boys and win awards, enhancing family pride. Fathers who are well educated themselves, in high status occupations, who have a range of leisure activities, find a sort of affinity and closeness with daughters who are able to respond to their ideas and concerns. This kind of dialogue was not attempted with their wives, perhaps for cultural reasons. Many fathers may not have been demonstrative or articulate in their affection or appreciation of their daughters, but somewhere in their hearts they have a soft spot for them, and this is something the writers of this book have discussed.

I was moved while reading this book. The writers have made a conscious effort to be detached and look at their relationships with their fathers. They tell us that whatever their talents or personalities, they have been nourished by their fathers. Many tell us candidly that their relationships were not always easy, or even fraught. There were differences of opinion, conflicts of interests, even neglect of their needs. Yet they have been able to distil what their fathers meant to them, what they did for them or what they did not do. Many admit it took considerable time to gain this understanding.

What comes through these writings is the fact of contradiction between a man as a father and a man as a husband. The loving, supportive, encouraging father is found to be ignoring, ill-treating, at times oppressive, towards the mother. During adolescence, many contributors did not perceive the relationship of father vis-à-vis mother to be problematic. Today, as discerning adults, they acknowledge the contradictions, and their accounts show the reality of the dichotomy between authoritarian/appreciative father and indifferent husband with lucidity and feeling. Perhaps the contributors could have explored the bundle of contradictory relationships that one lives with in the family as such to give a fuller picture? The editors tell us that they had deliberately decided to focus exclusively on the father-daughter relationship.

Indelible Imprints will contribute to growing concerns within society, within feminism, among those who distrust 'labels' but are self-questioning. It will certainly help us to understand the dynamics of personality building within patriarchal family structures. I am moved by the contributors' courage in facing certain truths about their lives and the charm of the simple, direct way that they write about their fathers. They have much to tell us.

Bombay, 1998 Neera Desai
Professor Emerita Sociology
SNDT Women's University, Bombay

Introduction

Why have a group of women got together to write about their fathers? We know that the relationship with our fathers is a significant one and marks us in ways that we can identify and in ways that we seem less aware of. Many of us had very complex relationships with our fathers, who traditionally have represented authority and access to the outside world with its promise of freedom. The first man in a daughter's life is her father, her introduction to the other sex. He is very special. The father-daughter relationship cannot be contained in definitions. The need to understand this relationship led us to an examination of ourselves as daughters: what drew us and bound us to our fathers? Our inquiry and search is expressed in our individual reflections collected in this book.

The first suggestion of writing about our fathers and ourselves came from Bindu Desai, many years ago. She had read a sensitive piece by Doris Lessing about her father that stayed with her for a long time, echoing in her mind. As memories swirled and surfaced, she was almost compelled to put them down. Talking about it with her sister Priti, she asked impulsively, 'Why don't we write about our fathers?' Priti and, later, Sonal were receptive and in November 1990, Bindu set out to write to eight friends, of whom Iqbal and Neela readily responded. And so we began.

As we sifted through experiences, recalled incidents, memorable moments, examined the interaction between father, the family, ourselves, to articulate what he meant to us, our efforts grew beyond mere biographical sketches. The qualitites that influenced us, the values that we absorbed and made our own, those that we rejected, the conflicting feelings of love and hurt, anguish, rage and fear. The need for father's approval and the elation when we won it, the bewilderment at being let down, the wrench at parting. These were shaky beginnings that we shared with each other hesitantly at our first meeting. Not all of us had come with something written. Neela had to wait for time to steady her emotions—her father's death was too recent—before she began. Iqbal demurred that her father had died when she was nineteen—it seemed so long ago. The response was enthusiastic, the empathy we felt at each other's narration, the familiarity of shared situations separated by time and distance. The contradictions that had baffled us then, that we bore with resentment gritted between teeth—we related these now with a touch of embarrassment. And to our surprise heard a chorus of 'me too', for others had had similar experiences, and we laughed together through our tears. It was a coming together of daughters who found themselves able to voice feelings and thoughts that had long lain undisturbed, almost forgotten. The atmosphere was so charged that we couldn't wait to get back to our writing, and those who had not started resolved to do so rightaway.

Over the next several months as we met and talked, our early hesitation, the mental blocks, the pain and resentment of the past gave way to an exploring and sharing of thoughts and notes. Reading our efforts together helped to clarify our ideas and emotions, focus our insights and perceptions. We chipped away diligently at layers of memory and suppressed feelings. When we discovered feet of clay, we accepted it as also our fathers contribution in shaping us and making us what we are. From these endeavours emerged the different facets of our fathers' personalities and behaviour as we completed our essays.

The five of us in the initial group—Bindu was visiting from America, and the others, Iqbal, Neela, Priti and Sonal in Bombay—found the exercise so stimulating, even challenging, that we decided to expand our circle. We asked others—friends, and friends of friends—to join us in our project. We did not seek out prominent personalities or those with special talents, though we did try to reach out to women from other regions and backgrounds. We sincerely believed that the theme being universal, it did not depend on the eminence of the father or the daughter. Among our contributors we have women who are writing for the first time along with others who are established writers. Some fathers were well known, others less so. As the group expanded, we found common denominators as well as differences. Most of us were university graduates from middle class families. We spoke many languages: Bengali, English, Gujarati, Hindi, Kannada, Punjabi, Tamil and Urdu. Our religious and cultural environments were varied: Christian, Hindu and Muslim. So were our ages, from Sarah at eighty-seven to Bindu born just after Independence. Different backgrounds, different experiences, different feelings.

Ours is not a structured study, written within the parameters of demographic, psychological or socioeconomic variables. We did not send out questionnaires or suggest a format for the contributions. Bindu's initial letter inviting us to write left the door wide open. No rules, no guidelines. We agreed that around 5000 words would be a good length. We had no deadlines except what we set ourselves. Exclusions, inclusions, were at the candour and discretion of the contributor. Our efforts are our recounting of part of our lives, though these do reflect individual interests and involvement in art, current affairs, media or women's issues. The contributions are intensely personal and the siblings barely get a look in for the writing focuses on father and self. Two sisters, Priti and Bindu—the eldest and the youngest among siblings—found themselves writing distinctly and separately about the same parent.

Born in the early years of this century, our fathers lived through the historic transition from colonial to independent India, spanning the decades of the struggle for freedom when society changed significantly. They were products of their times; for them education was the means to power and status in society. Events around them aroused contradictory ideas and conflicting emotions. Western influences of education and 'rationality' struggled against the constrictions of custom and tradition. There were pressures from family and society in the bringing up of daughters even if urban living provided some relief. And then there was the groundswell of patriotism and nationalist feeling. Perhaps, this was why fathers felt an irresistible urge to fashion their daughters into 'modern women'; a role that these men found difficult to imagine for their wives.

In our meetings to share the writing-in-progress we often discovered how supportive and encouraging fathers had been. This is a common thread, with just a few exceptions, that weaves through our portraits. True, they were autocratic, even overbearing at times, shaping the lives of their daughters—our lives. Yes, we admitted, as children we believed father was perfect; our adult sensibilities recognized his weaknesses and shortcomings. We were critical while also being more accommodating, forgiving. Though some of us had chafed at patriarchal protectiveness, at not being allowed to go out or travel alone, there was a general acceptance of father's authority as the head of the family, the fount of power. In some cases our fathers were not too ambitious for us, yet they enabled us to make the choices that the socio-political ferment threw up—in education, professional careers, choice of husband, finding space to express our identities. These were men who gave their daughters resolution and strength, despite the historical and cultural milieu that emphasized sons.

Essentially we wrote for ourselves and for each other. For many of us it was an enquiry into one's own life journey: 'How did I come to be what I am?' For Shyamala, writing in Connecticut, it was a catharsis, a healing process. Reflection and recounting let things fall into place. Perhaps Jane spoke for some of us when she wrote from Trivandrum that although she had rebelled against the constraints of her relationship with her father in her twenties, she accepts it now for it is a part of her. We discovered ourselves as we reached out to understand our fathers and came to terms with what had passed. Publication had not really been on our agenda. The idea of putting our reflections together in a book came later, out of a desire to share our explorations with other women, our sisterhood. And for our daughters and their daughters.

Our drafts completed, we each read all of the others. Mannu's moving manuscript was translated by Priti and Neela, checking back with her so that the shades of meaning, so beautiful in Hindi, were brought out as closely as possible. Sarah, our oldest contributor, was coaxed to remember and put down little incidents that seemed trivial to her but which greatly interested the rest of us. Comments, criticism, suggestions were given and minor changes made. There was the thrill of meeting contributors who had written from other cities and finding that the camaraderie of daughters had already made us good friends. We had to chase each other, deadlines were so often missed, manuscripts mislaid—it was all most enjoyable though it took us years to complete our project.

Our individual perspectives remain, our portraits vary: detailed, sketchy, disparate, passionate, detached, deeply felt, and we believe, always, truthful.

So here they are.

Bombay 1998   P.T.D., N.D., S.S.

Contents

Acknowledgments		vi
Foreword	Neera Desai	vii
Introduction	Priti T. Desai, Neera D'Souza and Sonal Shukla	xi
1 My Eyes Brim Over	Mannu Bhandari	1
2 Papa on the Swing	Bindu T. Desai	12
3 That Summer I Was Nineteen	Iqbal Monani	24
4 Out of the Top Drawer	Jane Pillai	37
5 Unfinished Business	Sonal Shukla	55
6 Let Colours Speak	Rekha Rao	67
7 Who Will Cherish Us Now?	Neela D'Souza	72
8 Bringing Him into Focus	Rinki Bhattacharya	88
9 My Invaluable Mentor	Priti T. Desai	95
10 Que Sera Sera	Sarah Major	108
11 Mixed Signals	Shyamala Ramayya Raman	115
12 Pressing the Wrong Nerve	Usha Kumar	126
List of Editors and Contributors		136

CHAPTER ONE

My Eyes Brim Over
Mannu Bhandari

From the time I was fourteen or fifteen right until I married Rajendr, I argued with Pitaji constantly over some matter or the other. As I try to rediscover my father today, more than thirty long years after his death, the rage of those days has quietened, and it is with a detached mind and insight that I view him. Not just the outward facade, what he appeared to be, but the man within, with all his contradictions, compulsions, weaknesses.

To bring my recollections of Pitaji into focus I reach far back into time and see the two-storey house in Ajmer. The upper storey was his domain. There he reclined on a mattress, propped up with bolsters and cushions, reading or dictating with a mess of papers, books and magazines strewn around him. Downstairs, with all of us brothers and sisters, was Ma, our uneducated, identityless mother, her wifely status reduced to one of subservience to the dawn to dusk demands of the household, eagerly ministering to Pitaji's every need and desire, however trifling.

Before moving to Ajmer, Pitaji lived in Indore where he was well known. He was associated with the Congress party and also actively involved in welfare work and had connections with one or two newspapers. He was a man of standing and his name commanded respect. Pitaji ardently supported education and held forth on its many advantages; this was no mere rhetoric for he sheltered and educated about a dozen students in our house, some of whom later attained high positions. Those were his happiest days and his generosity was boundless. But all this was hearsay. The father I knew was a man weighed down by adversity, clinging to traces of that former life. Sensitive and soft-hearted, he was also proud and had a fiery temper. Pitaji would not bow to anyone nor would he compromise. To the end he remained himself, egotistical and arrogant, even through the awful dark and dismal days of economic hardship. An unexpected reversal in his fortunes had uprooted him from Indore and forced him to move to Ajmer. And it was here that he arranged his eldest daughter's marriage. I barely remember my sister's wedding. Till then, except for acknowledging him as my father, I had no real bonds of attachment to him.

The first impression of Pitaji that registered strongly in my mind and sank deep into my subconscious was that I was fit only to be neglected by him. He was partial to a fair skin. I was dark, skinny, listless. Even today I well recall my good-looking, fair sister with her cheerful smile. She was two years older than me, and in comparison to her all I got were looks that spelt indifference, even distaste. Listening to my sister being praised for whatever she did deepened my feelings of worthlessness, of being shut out from his world. Did I not cry out for attention? My mulish obstinacy over little matters, my childish tantrums, did they not reveal my inner agony? Yet he never noticed, never understood. Those were not days when each child received individual parental attention. Every family had half a dozen children who grew up with each other in their own world, separate from the adults, as did we five siblings.

Even today I remember Pitaji, having bathed and breakfasted early, disappearing upstairs as we left for school. What was he doing there? We were too young for curiosity or the need to know. It was much later that I learnt that he was at work on an English-Hindi lexicon, *The Twentieth Century English-Hindi Dictionary*, his life's magnum opus and a unique venture at that time. Its publication brought him fame and prestige. Pandit Nehru, Dr. Rajendra Prasad, Madan Mohan Malaviya, leaders, scholars, distinguished literati and academicians acknowledged and applauded his outstanding contribution. He found his lost worth, came into his own, it was his supreme hour! On a promotional tour his arrival in Calcutta was reported by newspapers; he kept these clippings carefully; indeed, he saved anything printed anywhere about his dictionary. Along with them were stored congratulatory messages that he had received. He hoarded these treasures and displayed them with great pride to visitors; occasionally, he would read them aloud and explain them to us too.

Pitaji not only compiled the dictionary himself but also handled the sales. Our home was his office, and all the members of the household his staff. We two sisters did our bit enthusiastically—

pinning the pages of the introductory letter, folding and inserting it into envelopes and sticking the stamps—without the faintest idea about the importance of his work. It had meaning for us only on the rare days that brought us gifts and unexpected pleasures. A new film at the local theatre and my brothers would wait to catch him in a relaxed mood and seize the opportunity to get his permission to see it. Oh, the excitement of the cinema! I remember the thrill that lingered on for three or four days thereafter. But I do not remember if Pitaji ever saw a film himself. Maybe he did see *Sant Gyaneshwar* and *Sant Tulsidas*.

In 1944, right after she passed her Matric at the age of sixteen, my sister was married off; the following year, both my brothers, who had finished their Masters' degrees, got married. I was fifteen when the sheltering canopy of sibling camaraderie folded up. And that was when my real relationship with Pitaji began. When he dispensed homeopathic medicines free to the neighbourhood, I was more than just his compounder; he explained what he prescribed and why he chose that specific medicine. When a sick person arrived, he would consult me on what to give him. When someone with a serious ailment got better with his prescription, Pitaji would be happier than the patient and would continue to discuss the details of the case till the end of the day. If it happened that the typist took leave, I would write Pitaji's letters by hand. Still, in those days, he would not permit me to go out of the *mohalla* on my own. My brothers' friends would come from time to time to run errands or to help me with my homework. Though Pitaji did not like them being around, he did not embarrass me with a foolish suggestion that I make them my *rakhi* brothers—that surely would have earned us both ridicule. Whenever politicians gathered at our home he insisted that I sit with him, listen to their discussions and get to know what was happening in the country.

Discussions and debates were his favourite pastime; many a time he debated issues with me, as long as I went along with his views. Any disagreement upset him. It was then that I began to argue with him and even oppose him on every little issue. Perhaps, he forgot that, after all, this adversary who stuck so obstinately to her point was his own daughter. Discussions, arguments, of these we had plenty, yet I do not remember that we children ever sat and talked to him of our own personal feelings, dilemmas, problems. No, despite his 'modernism' he was totally a tradition-bound father, overbearing and commanding, a man of refinement but, nevertheless, a patriarch who distanced himself especially from his daughters. And, of course, our ordinary daily matters never held any interest for him. We would go to him with our progress reports from school. Without noticing where we stood in the class he would sign them, saying, 'Come first... work harder... I only want to see you stand first...'.

I remember vividly the first day of my Matric examination. Pitaji was coming down the stairs and noticed Ma serving me *peda* and *dahi*. When she explained that I was about to leave for my exam, he was taken aback. '*Arre*, when did you get into the Tenth Standard? I didn't even know!' Perhaps, in those days most families treated their children rather casually, quite unlike today's parents, who concentrate all their attention on them.

Pacing up and down the verandah, or around the courtyard, as was his habit, he would be murmuring to himself, going over his thoughts, occasionally raising his arms in a gesture as if he were addressing an audience. I wondered what ideas and plans were bubbling in his mind, waiting to be expressed in words. Ma would call out, 'Your clothes have been put in the bathroom, go and bathe.' In a dazed voice he would exclaim, 'Oh, so I haven't bathed?' We would burst out laughing and joining in our laughter he would rush off to the bathroom. He really had to be told to have a bath, reminded to have his meal. Thinking about those days, I am amazed that Ma, who always trembled at his anger, could also look after him as though he were a child.

From passively listening to the problems of the nation, when I entered college next year I became an active participant in events around me. Pitaji was confronted by an unexpected hazard. His ideas of modernity limited me to being a discerning listener at home, it did not permit me the freedom to be out in the world. The thought of his daughter being friendly with boys and going around with them was intolerable. But 1947 was approaching and could you be content, confined at home? *Prabhatpheris*, strikes, demonstrations, speeches aroused and galvanized every city. Young people passionately desired to prove their mettle. Patriotism surged in our veins, inflaming us. I would leave home early every morning and slip back quietly after dark. If this was not enough to anger him, matters were made worse when someone reported that I was out all day. 'Striding along the streets, gesturing, shouting slogans—and in the company of boys! Does this speak well for the daughter of this house?' Only too aware of his social standing, Pitaji was not ready for such intransigence. Luckily, the very next day Dr. Ambalalji, Pitaji's close friend and a well-known figure in Ajmer, came home and greeted me with a hearty pat on the back. 'What a speech Mannu made yesterday! You should have been there to hear your daughter's eloquence. I am really proud of her.' Pitaji's anger melted away. Could it be that he too felt proud of me?

It was during that time that a letter arrived from my college principal: 'Your daughter is responsible for the indiscipline in the college. Please see me immediately or—' Pitaji hit the roof. 'Till this day I have never been told off on account of my children. What further humiliation is in store for me because of you?' But in the list of misdeeds that the principal had elaborated, one sentence was my salvation. 'We try our best to maintain discipline and start the class. But she just has to spread the word to leave and the room empties at once. No one is left. Today the whole college responds to the whims of these few girls. Somehow or the other, please keep her at home, if not—' What Pitaji said to the principal I don't know, but when he returned home he was not angry but seemed rather pleased that his daughter Mannu was clearly the ringleader among those girls. Young as I was, I realized that to be outstanding, to be in the forefront, mattered more to Pitaji than anything else. For him, that spelt success. Fame was his greatest ambition, his weakness too.

Pitaji was not one for religious rituals. The marriages of his children were duties he had to carry out, and as far as I can recall, they took place without fuss and celebration. He did not think music, dancing and other traditional rituals were necessary—or did financial restraints hold him back? Wedding arrangements were supervised by his brothers, as Pitaji knew little of what had to be done and nothing of organization. Divali was a cultural event celebrated with great enthusiasm; we children joyfully lit the *diyas* while Ma worked diligently in the kitchen to cook all the wonderful delicacies that were expected of her. But I never saw any religious celebrations at home.

Pitaji had studied the Jain scriptures in depth. Though he was of the faith he never fasted, or observed festivals and there were no visits to temples for *darshan*. I do not remember Pitaji bowing to any deity. Religion was not inculcated in us. Once a group of Jain nuns on a pilgrimage camped overnight at our home. Ma was ecstatic. Our large front yard was full of devotees but Pitaji would not even come down. 'These women who do not know even the basics of Jainism, you think I would come down to see them?' I joined the gathering in the yard and was so argumentative that Ma was quite unhappy. But when Pitaji heard about it he was delighted.

It was a day to celebrate—the arrival of a new section of the dictionary from the printers. With great enthusiasm he would see to the wrapping and labelling of the parcels. After they were dispatched he would distribute sweets all around. Perhaps this took the place of a religious celebration for him, a festival day. His face happy, he truly radiated joy. A different father emerged from within him—loving, tender, ready to banter and laugh with every one—ready to fulfil every desire, a generous-hearted father. His affection was evident again when anyone was sick; he would be at the bedside all the time, comforting, reassuring, gently stroking the forehead.

After independence, conditions changed rapidly. The popularity of the dictionary was no longer the same. His economic situation worsened, social relationships were disturbed. There is one incident that I cannot forget. A recommendation letter from Pitaji had enabled a person to get a teacher's post on a salary of Rs.15 in Indore. Now the same man was a minister in the state government. During a visit to Ajmer the man did not even call on Pitaji. Outwardly, Pitaji was composed and seemed indifferent but we could see the torment of his agonized waiting as long as the minister was in town. When the man left Ajmer, Pitaji seethed impotently, unable to express his rage. He knew very well that had he gone to the minister and dropped even the slightest hint, the man may well have helped in the sale of the dictionary. But Pitaji's ego would not permit this, as much as the minister's ego would not permit him to help without his favour first being sought!

I experienced Pitaji's stubborn pride when I applied for a teaching position at Vanasthali. This was just after I had completed my M.A. He found it intolerable that I should be applying there as the founders and administrators of Vanasthali were all people he knew, so he insisted that I should leave blank the column under 'Father's name' in my application form, as he did not want his name to figure in it. I complied. I was furious at his lack of sympathy and cooperation, and only now I realize it wasn't that: the thought that a daughter of his might have to ask a favour from his friends and acquaintances deeply hurt his ego. What transpired, and why I rejected a telegraphic appointment offer—all that is another story.

Pitaji never sought favours or help. It was no surprise for us when he returned empty-handed after a meeting with Pandit Nehru. He had been granted a ten minute audience, but Panditji spent twenty minutes with him, praising Pitaji and the dictionary. Pitaji came away walking on air. The friend who had arranged the meeting shook his head in disgust. 'When Nehru praised you, that was the cue; he would have given you substantial help for the dictionary if you had only asked. Well, now you have his praise to sustain you and see you through your difficulties.' Pitaji had no regrets. He had the satisfaction that he had not stooped to ask a favour.

Through out his life Pitaji wore only khadi kurtas and pyjamas; for an occasion he would sport a *bandh-gala* khadi coat. The only luxury our home had was a small table fan which was always near him. For entertainment we had a radio. Decorative articles and even those for comfort or convenience did not attract him nor did he consider them necessary. He had no addictions other than the two *paans* he ate every day. Yet, a servant had to be at his beck and call, when he was at home as well as when he travelled: to unpack the holdall, to open the tiffin box or insert the drawstring in his pyjamas—these tasks were beyond him. At home he could not so much as fetch himself a glass of water or wash his shaving gear. In addition to Ma, who worked as hard as two servants, a servant was a necessity for Pitaji. Feudalism was dead, but the habit of being waited upon like royalty was ingrained in him.

His personal expenses covered newspapers, magazines and books, but the expenses of social living, offering hospitality to guests, were far beyond his capacity. A warm welcome, the serving of choice food—that was part of him, almost second nature. Perhaps, it made him happy too. I don't know why but I always suspected that he wanted to be lauded for his large-heartedness, his generosity. Ma silently accepted all this, never opposing him, but seeing her burdened by his hospitality enraged me. And, most of all, I seethed at all this expenditure on feeding others. After all, didn't we have needs, desires? Why were these never attended to?

An incident I vividly remember: Mr. Panikkar of the Communist party turned up one day and hesitantly asked for Rs.10. Just two days before that I had been forbidden to buy chappals. Ma too had timidly expressed her fears about expenses and that money was scarce. But Pitaji insisted on helping Panikkar. My tears brought a reprimand, 'If someone comes home asking for help, you do not send him away empty-handed. I'll buy you new chappals, till then why don't you have the old ones mended?' I could never understand why our wishes and needs were so low down in his priorities, especially when we were short of money. Indeed, as our financial situation worsened, he seemed to forget me altogether. In 1947 I passed the Intermediate but with troubles in the college, my education was interrupted; later I did the B.A. and M.A. as a private student. These single-handed efforts to educate myself brought me no support or encouragement from Pitaji—he wasn't even interested. Why was he so harsh towards me, his daughter, when he had educated children of others at his own expense? Resentment and anger tormented me. Slowly, over the years, came a resigned acceptance.

After finishing my master's degree I went to Calcutta to explore the possibilities of research and met Dr. Lalitprasad Shukla who, on hearing my name, burst out, 'But you are the daughter of a distinguished father!' Again after my marriage, when Bai (mother-in-law) took me to visit a respected elder citizen of Agra, the reaction was similar, 'Tarabai, your home is graced by the daughter of a famous and noble man.' I wondered sadly if I or my brothers or my mother figured anywhere in this impression of greatness and nobility.

Towards his servants Pitaji was exceedingly compassionate and sensitive. Then why did he show such callousness towards Ma? Ma who had reduced herself to almost nothing, her only purpose in life to serve him. My sister had married at sixteen and moved away from home, but my brothers and I did not have an easy spontaneous relationship with him. My anger against Pitaji mounted. Looking back today, I wonder. There are men whose aims and expectations are not constricted by family and parochial considerations, who reach out to the world. Their generosity and love enfolds humanity. Of course, the immediate family suffers neglect and indifference—as we well knew from our experience. I now accept that Pitaji belonged to that select breed.

With government sponsorship and funding, several committees worked on many different dictionaries, and Pitaji's own lexicon lost its appeal and eminence. While his colleagues were prospering and achieving important positions, isolated as he was by his own principles and ego, Pitaji grew more aloof and lonely. He wrote his *History of India's Freedom Struggle* at this time but it did not have an impact. Day by day his economic situation worsened, numbing his sensibilities, making him so withdrawn and self-centred that he did not realize that I was well past the marriageable age, that I too had emotional and physical needs—that as my father he had responsibilities towards me.

I was home in Ajmer for the holidays when my eternally burdened and harassed Ma brought up the subject of my marriage. Pitaji directed his anger at my brothers who had failed in their duty, for they should have taken the responsibility for this sister of theirs. When I was twenty-eight and had got to know Rajendr, my sister came to Ajmer to broach the subject of marriage. Pitaji not only opposed it but was so outraged that right up to the day of my wedding he bombarded me with telegrams to call off the marriage. All through his life Pitaji had declared himself against the divisions of caste and creed—now he seemed a hypocrite and an uncaring one at that. I married without his blessings, my heart full of bitterness towards him.

I don't know why, but on reflection I wonder if it was Rajendra's profession as a freelance writer that aroused Pitaji's ire. If at that time he had had the recognition and the status he has now, Pitaji would have accepted him whole-heartedly. How well Pitaji knew that the lack of sound financial backing thwarts brilliance and competence, causing relationships to break and wither away. Maybe he wanted to save me those agonies, or maybe being hard-pressed and with his fame fading, he no longer had the courage to face criticisms of my decision to marry a Yadav. Be it as it may, my bitter feelings dissolved only after our last meeting.

Two-and-a-half years after my marriage a hand-written postcard arrived—a summons from Pitaji. A few days earlier I had come to know that he was suffering from cancer of the oesophagus. The doctors at the Tata Hospital had decided not to operate, and he was now with my elder brother in Indore. All through the long journey there I wondered if Pitaji, who held his head high always, would now be cowed by death. He would flinch at the slightest discomfort, even a 99°F temperature—how could he bear the agonizing pain of cancer?

When I reached Indore, he seemed quite normal, pacing up and down the verandah like the Pitaji of old. I felt relieved. By evening I sensed that he was not at ease here; his pride and self-respect did not allow him to be happy in another home, even if it happened to be his son's. The doctors had given him only six to eight months more; he took up the challenge, asked for books and journals on cancer and started to work on his health. Lying in bed at night, he confided to me, 'Mannu, I want just five more years of life, only five more . . . so that I can have my encyclopaedia printed. Believe me, it will be a landmark.' Then pointing towards a box under his bed which contained the manuscript of his encyclopaedia, he continued, 'That holds six years of labour . . . six years . . .' Suddenly, silence. He was staring at the ceiling. Who knows, even in those crucial last days of his life, was his mind dreaming of the prestige that his *viswakosh* would bring?

After a while he wanted me to take down his cloth bag—the old familiar *thela* which contained his reviews, letters of praise and a whole bunch of press clippings—the *thela* which I had ingenuously embroidered. He pressed into my hands a letter from Dr. Rajendra Prasad expressing concern at his illness and wishing him recovery and good health. Pitaji's face wore a contented look and I could glimpse a hint of pride. 'Others do not know, or else they too would have written.' With this letter as anchor, I felt he was reassuring himself that he had retained his fame and prestige, that people looked up to him. After reading it, I gave the letter back to him; he carefully put it away in his *thela* and then lay down. And I reflected that the dignity, honour, fame of his entire life had been compressed into this *thela*, that was his past, his pride was stored in it. His future, his dreams were safe in the box under the bed—dreams that would not see fulfillment. Deep within me I dissolved into sadness and got up and went indoors. I stayed a fortnight with Pitaji and returned home.

Three months later when the oesophagus was blocked, he was removed to a nursing home. He read the newspapers unfailingly every day. The Chinese invasion and India's vulnerability demoralized him more than his own condition. The day before he died, hearing the news, he whispered weakly, 'Looks like Nehru will take the country into hell.' Those were his last words. No invoking

Ram, no call to God. After that he lost his voice and his consciousness. Early next day, before dawn, his spirit soared free.

I asked my brother, just back from Indore, 'Before he died, did Pitaji even once ask Ma's forgiveness for a lifetime of harshness? If not in words, at least by an affectionate gesture, a tender touch? Did he remember his daughters?' No, he had not asked, he had not remembered. In the vastness of his concern for his country, we, his family, had no place. He had no land, no house, no wealth, no bank balance to leave behind. His only legacy was his library—the collection of a lifetime. He had asked us to donate all his books to the Indore Public Library. So after his death the books were sent there. His death was announced on both the prime time news broadcasts. If only he could have heard them somehow, somewhere his yearnings for fame and success may have been satisfied.

I do not remember weeping at his death. And yet, as I write these pages, my eyes brim over.

NOTE
This piece was written in Hindi by the author and translated into English by Priti T. Desai and Neela D'Souza.

Chapter Two

Papa on the Swing
Bindu T. Desai

These reflections about my father are written as an inquiry into my own life's journey. How did I become what I am? It came together vividly when my sister Jyoti and I were shopping at an Indian grocery store in America. Two Indian men were there too. Both wore braces or 'suspenders' as the Americans say. It triggered off a chain of thought in my mind, and indeed I remarked to Jyoti at the time, how I living in the West for nearly two decades often wore Indian clothes and yet how Papa had been such a dandy even by Western standards, certainly by American ones. Was this because of a need to belong to a group seen as having power? Curious in an age when this power, European colonial power, was challenged everywhere and on all fronts; the challenge symbolized by clothes too; from the uniforms of the Red Army in the Russian Revolution, to the Mao jackets, to our own Gandhi cap and *khadidhari*. Why did Papa want to look like a saheb? An upper class one at that, waistcoat, bow ties, felt hat, the garb of well-to-do financiers and insurance men? He was expressing something by his clothes, he was fairly fastidious about them.

My father was born in 1905 in Surat, the youngest son in a family of six children and given the name Khandubhai. He was a dark-skinned, quiet child, often carried around by his elder sister on her hip. His mother was most unusual for that time—she was older than her husband and had been to school up to the Seventh Standard, and was overbearing, temperamental, difficult to please, arrogant and hurtful. My mother recalls her with anger, even hate. My grandfather, fair and handsome, was a school teacher who moved to Bombay and later became a principal of a high school. A stern disciplinarian at work and at home, he beat his children at the slightest pretext. Khandu hated these thrashings and must have vowed never to beat his own kids. This promise Papa kept—he never beat us. Somewhere Papa decided Khandubhai was too old-fashioned a name and changed his name to Thakorebhai and it was as Thakore or TK that he was known all his life.

He grew up to be a hard-working, ambitious, modern man academically brilliant, graduating in law and arts from the University of Bombay. At twenty-two he married Kusum, a large eyed, short, exceedingly handsome girl of fifteen. She remembers her first glimpse of him—he had a red shawl draped on his shoulders and far too much oil in his hair. Bespectacled, he did not look at all like her idea of a husband.

He was selected as a management trainee by an insurance company and as part of being groomed for bigger and better things, was sent to England in 1929. There is a picture of him, slim, tall, hair neatly combed in place, standing with his arms around my mother's shoulder, a slight smile tinged with amusement at her shyness forming on his face. He wore stylish European suits, immaculately tailored. He read voraciously, and browsing at new, and second-hand bookshops was a pleasurable hobby all his life. He bought books on cricket, horse racing, economics, history, plays and also every English newspaper that came out in Bombay.

England was followed by stints in Lahore and Madras. Lahore must have been a very happy time for he was able to establish his own household, away from the joint family Kusum knew in Bombay. He was keen to live well and gradually acquired all the airs of a feudal lord without caring to secure the material basis necessary for the role! Papa was doing well and when he moved to Bombay he naturally looked beyond his family's two-room flat in an overcrowded locality. He located a spacious ground floor flat, which he rented for Rs.105 in 1935, a princely sum then, and now, perhaps, the most substantive material legacy he has left his daughters who continue to live there.

His first child, a daughter, Priti, was born in 1934. Later came Kalindi, Sita, Jyoti, Asit and lastly, in 1948, me. My first memory of him is set in a comfortable home and a chauffeur-driven car. I remember running from his bedroom many a time. He had just come out of his bath wrapped in a towel which he let fall, revealing what to me seemed interesting parts—the thicket of pubic hair and genitals covered matter-of-factly by underpants. He was totally unselfconscious. Then the trousers zippered, shirt tucked in, cuff links, leather belt, tie and socks in hand, he would go out to the front room to his favourite perch. This was a bench swing with an enormous pillow on it which he used as a desktop, scribbling away on his pad, one leg kicking the ground, cigarette always in hand, the ash dropping on the other side and gathered up by Gangaram during the two daily sweepings the house got. Morning began with a tray of tea taken out to Papa—two to three cups all poured and ready to go. While he liked good food he was never fastidious about it being piping hot and ate everything set in front of him without complaint. He was a big man in the early fifties, youthful slimness being replaced by a beer belly, and weighed over 200 pounds.

My earliest memories of childhood—a big old radio, after which came other electrical gadgets. Papa bought a second-hand fan for the dining room. Mummy grumbled, 'Always second-hand things, he loves second-hand things.' Some of this anger over second-hand things might also have referred to his mistresses.

Mummy was keen that her younger kids go to an English-medium school, she being among the first of her generation to want what was till then a preserve of the brown sahebs—setting a trend that became a flood within her circle of Gujarati women.

He was a kind father to me—only once did he beat me. It all started because I hated going to school and refused to do whatever my nursery teacher wanted. And so when Papa came home from work, Mummy told him how naughty I was, how I did not study and how I needed disciplining. He glared at her and asked for a ruler. It was brought out and he held both my hands in one of his and with the other struck my petticoat with the ruler and sternly asked me to study. I sobbed loudly but from then on I knew he and I shared a secret—he only hit the flare of my petticoat, taking care not to hurt me. I understood our comradeship. It was a very special day—he never had to scold me about studying again. Later that year I told him I had come first in class. He gave me a five-rupee note and when it turned out that I had actually ranked sixth, he did not demand it back. I remembered and liked that. Once my siblings had gone out for a *paan* that I particularly liked—ice cold, dipped in a pleasantly sweet syrup—and it cost just an anna. They returned from this treat without getting one for me. When Papa came home I was crying. He asked me why and said right away, 'Don't worry—here take some money for *paan*', and, gave me all the change he had, 5 annas (for 5 *paans!*) and a diary from his briefcase. I was thrilled.

He often went away on business trips: to Calcutta from where he would get a tin of rosogollas for me, to Europe from where he got us a train set, some toy cars and Bavarian dolls. His trips to Europe were long—six to eight weeks sometimes—and when we were very boisterous, Mummy would threaten to write to him for a whip to discipline us. As trip followed trip and no whip ever materialized we began to realize that Mummy's threats held no substance. He would come back from Europe laden with chocolates. He loved being greeted at the airport and with a rosogolla tin or other such prize awaiting me, I was nearly always at hand to receive him—even if he'd only been on a two-or three-day trip to Calcutta. Indeed, it was the threat of a policeman arresting me at the airport if I had dirty hair (I hated getting my hair washed, the soap in my eyes bothered me no end) that got me to agree to Mummy's washing my hair. I was so keen to go to the airport that once I went without any panties on, and Pritiben had to carry me in a discreet manner so that I wouldn't reveal my bare bottom!

As Mummy refused to go with him to social functions like weddings of business colleagues or their relatives, he would take me. He was always very well groomed. For a wedding: a well-pressed suit, a sprinkling of Chanel No.5—I have a weakness for Chanel No.5 even now—suspenders, brightly polished brown or black shoes, sometimes a cigarette, sometimes a cigar and the two of us were off. I was the cynosure of all eyes, being the Big Boss's daughter. I got to eat two or three plates of ice cream—no Mummy around to warn me of teeth falling out—and he could show me off. He'd work the crowd, as the Americans say, cigarette in hand, waving and gesticulating as he spoke with swarms of younger officials hanging on to every word and laughing loudly at his jokes.

One Sunday when the others had gone to Elephanta for a picnic discarding me as being a nuisance, he and Mummy took me to the Gymkhana Races. It was a wonderful afternoon. I went to the paddocks, to Papa's box and when coming home he took me for ice cream, laughingly brushing away my suggestion that we drop Mummy home because she wouldn't let us eat as much as we'd like! The racing season meant a rupee given to each of us before he went. The others bought pastries. I saved my rupee and found that I had, over three to four seasons, saved nearly three hundred rupees, which I kept folded in a brass box. Mummy later borrowed this money from me, so it did come in useful in a way.

The years 1953, 1954 and 1955 were carefree. Monsoon Sundays meant long drives. When we reached Khopoli at the foot of the Western Ghats I would recite my jingle

> Coca-Cola, Coca-Cola not to be drunk by me
> The water from the *matka* has filled my belly.

Of course, Mummy had insisted we drink water before leaving home and not demand Coca-Cola. Papa would roar with laughter at this jingle, and Coca-Cola always won out.

Cricket was a passion with Papa. We went to test matches—all five of us. He loved all sports, though he only played bridge, and flew a kite with skill. We went to football games, hockey matches and wrestling bouts. He loved festivals too. For Sankranti, kites were ordered from Surat as was the *manja*, the deadly powdered-glass reinforced string. He was an indulgent parent in so many ways.

He loved his drink, a peg every day. He had decanters, hip flasks, you name it. Watching him, I once demanded some too and he said affectionately, 'Go get a glass,' and poured me a bit, and this then became a routine. On holiday in Mount Abu, where I saw a man being led away by the police because he had been drinking, my six-year-old voice burst forth indignantly, 'But my father drinks every day and no one arrests him.'

Approaching his fifties, there he was, proudly proclaimed by his friends as the uncrowned king of the insurance industry. The crown was to elude him forever. He had worked for New India Assurance for thirty years, never taking a day of sick or privilege leave. The company was everything to him. It had recognized his brilliance, given him power and influence. He loved New India. He was loyal to it as he was to his children, perhaps even more so. He was deluged with offers to join other companies but passed them over. He seemed to have understood well corporate power—the power that highly placed executives have. He loved to train, to teach, to instruct. He trained the first batch of women managers in the Indian insurance industry; today they have risen to head companies themselves. A hard taskmaster, he had a reputation for fairness, for sticking his neck out for a junior. Once there had been a big loss. His junior whose fault it was, explained the matter to him, expecting to be dismissed, but Papa grunted and said, 'Do not worry, I okayed it too, I will take the blame', and that was that. This incident gave him a reputation of almost legendary proportions. He was generous to his staff. At company functions he would refuse food till he had checked whether the chauffeur and peons had been fed (he might have done this only once but that event marked him). Yes, they did care for him, for they came to check on his health when he had no power to wield.

In his community and his family he aroused envy and commanded grudging respect. A few came to him looking for jobs. Even I, at the age of six, realized these were supplicants from the way Papa barely acknowledged their existence and from Mummy's embarrassment at Papa's behaviour. Mummy would offer them tea and after a mumbled greeting go back in. Papa swung away, not a word was exchanged. The visitors would read the newspapers lying around and would return day after day till finally one morning Papa might grunt, 'Tell him to go to the Company tomorrow.' He did some favours here and there but his brusque and even imperious manner meant he got no affection in return. In an odd way, I think this is what he might have appreciated the most. He dismissed most of his relatives as gossip-mongers and barely exchanged a word with them.

There are other memories of Papa—his card games. Come Saturday afternoon, the drawing room would be emptied of all furniture and mattresses spread over the floor. Several friends would come to play bridge, which went on till late at night. Mummy would serve snacks and of course lots of tea. Then Papa on other Saturdays, forever trying to catch BBC's 'Sports Round Up', moving the dial constantly in an unceasing effort to get the best reception.

In early 1956 Papa was upset because a close colleague had lost the faculty of speech after a stroke. Was he apprehensive about his own long neglected diabetes and high blood pressure? I recall an abscess on Papa's hip that took very long to heal. Then came that fateful Friday—3 August. I vividly remember that evening. He had come home and soon was setting off somewhere and I, as an eight year old sensed it was somewhere he should not be going. (I learnt much later that he had gone to his mistress's flat.) His foot dragged as he went down the steps and he brushed off assistance. Perhaps, because he was not feeling well he came home early that night. My brother, Asit, noticed something wrong and exclaimed to Mummy as Papa lay down to rest for the night,

'Mummy, look! Papa's face is funny.' It was being pulled to one side. Our family doctor was sent for. He said it was the beginning of a paralytic stroke. Morning saw a Papa who needed help going to the bathroom and who couldn't hold a cigarette in his hand. That Saturday was a long one. So many people came, so many cars parked on our narrow street, someone thought it was Pritiben's engagement. Asit and I played in the garden or hung around our mother, hearing her repeat for the tenth time what had happened. Several specialists examined Papa and by late afternoon he was admitted to a nursing home.

Life was never the same again. The sole earning member of our family of seven was felled by a stroke that made the right side of his body virtually useless. His speech was spared. It was a little slurred initially. His speech and the facial twist got better fairly quickly. He had superb medical care; yet it was like locking the stable after the horse had bolted. Now that I am a neurologist and I look back, I can see that he was asking for it. He was an untreated hypertensive, diabetic, grossly overweight and a chain-smoker—fingers and nails stained with nicotine.

And so, with this stroke he began to pay for all the liberties he had taken, big and small. A man who rarely stayed at home, he was now more or less confined to the house. From a chain-smoker and steady heavy drinker, overnight he became a teetotaller and non-smoker. Overnight, his family was exposed to the absence of material security. No savings, no money to pay hospital bills, loans from friends to be honoured and the prospect of no income, once his sick leave was over. There was Mummy, who had never written a cheque in her life, who never suspected he had been so cavalier with her children's security and hers, whose dowry, had he saved it, would have been substantial. All gone in irresponsible overspending, and here she was at forty-four, having to reap the harvest of his mistakes, his rakishness, his liabilities. And so Mummy took the reins of the family in her hands, and with the help of a few faithful friends paid back the creditors and wondered what the future might hold.

Slowly Papa got better. The newly opened Physiotherapy Department at KEM Hospital sent its best student to help him. He started to walk again, footsteps being marked on the front room, holding onto a thick rope. Gradually he was able to walk by himself at home and needed a stick only when he went out. A few months after his stroke, he went to his New India office and was mobbed by colleagues and juniors. Had the company wanted to, they could have kept him on but he was retired prematurely. Only the barest that was his due was given. His car was withdrawn. His annuity was to be paid till his son turned twenty-one. The reality of material insecurity sank deep into the consciousness of all five of us, yet in some ways we all lived better than before. A Swiss associate whose career Papa must have furthered indirectly arranged for a consultancy, and though Papa's earnings were much less now, in Mummy's sensible care, the family never knew want. We were able to continue in the expensive schools we had been admitted to and occasionally went on holidays in the Himalayas.

Mummy had a special swing designed for him, a chair with handles, deeply cushioned with a movable footrest for him to place his paralyzed right foot while he swung away kicking with his left. Papa never sought pity. In the sixteen years he lived after his stroke, rarely did he comment on his disability. Yes, the early period was stormy as he railed against a fate that had left him paralyzed and dependent on a wife he knew he had wronged and children whose future he had not provided for. His fury was great. He fought with his nurses, his therapists, his nursing aides. The wounds healed as he too healed, and Mummy, what did she not try to make him well again! All kinds of splints were tied, all kinds of oils massaged, pilgrimages made, fasts undertaken, concoctions brewed, *vaidyas* and quacks consulted, her deep faith giving Mummy a serenity rationality could never provide. Slowly a new pattern of life emerged at home and Papa, who could very easily have died, now had time to savour and see his children grow.

I took him for his first movie after his stroke. We went to see *23 Paces to Baker Street* and enjoyed it enormously. It brought back memories of London. He did not talk about himself very much, indeed in the sixteen years he lived after his stroke, he rarely reminisced about his past: no regrets, no self-pity, few reflections, sometimes flashes of insights into colleagues, but that, too, seldom.

Though confined to the house physically, his world expanded. He quickly seemed to have absorbed that one way to make his days enjoyable would be to share in others' joys. This he did, unobtrusively and gradually. For a neighbour's daughter who dreamt about film stars, he saved old film magazine articles; for another who cared about politics he kept news items; for the cricket fans there were *Wisdens* to talk about. For a few years he even had a part-time job. He went for an hour to a small insurance company as an adviser. Now he was the epitome of warmth and social grace to anyone who dropped in.

Mummy and he had a trait I never realized or credited them with, till my cousin pointed it out to me some decades later. They always listened to what we had to say. Any remark, any observation was interesting. We were never snubbed or cut to size. Outrageous remarks were often greeted by Papa with exuberant laughter. I was (am) a regular chatterbox. On long drives in the car Papa would promise me a four-anna coin if I kept quiet for five minutes. I never could and he would chuckle with happiness for he never lost one four-anna bit. When I dropped off to sleep on the way back home he would say, 'The first wicket has fallen.'

In 1958 he had a setback. He had gone out for a walk on a very rainy day. Most people would have stayed at home but he said he could not bear just to sit in the house. He slipped and fell, fractured his femur. It was eight months before Papa was able to walk again. In 1964, sitting for several hours at a stretch while Asit went through his sacred thread ceremony, Papa had another stroke, luckily on the same side as before. His right leg became weaker and he now needed a crutch even at home. He did most things himself but needed someone to give him a bath and to pour water so that he could wash his hands after his meals. Other than that he needed no care. The arm rest of his swing became a favourite seat for many, the neighbourhood kids, for Asit and me. Sometimes I would sit and nuzzle him on his cheek and he would say, *'maro dayo dikko che'* (my smart little child).

For a few years after his stroke several business colleagues would come home, some to seek advice about their work, others to look him up. Gradually the numbers dwindled. As we grew, our friends coming to see us took over as his own friends had quietly slipped 'into death's dateless night'. The years went by and it so happened that none of his daughters married. He never once remarked about this, but he did say that on one leg and with one arm he was hardly going to be able to find husbands for his daughters! He worried about Sita, my sister with a cleft palate, and so anxious was he about her academic abilities that he asked someone to double check her results in the SSC! Priti was his right hand, closer to him than any of us, and he was immensely proud of her.

That was a lovely monsoon, in 1961, Jyoti and Asit both joining college, and suddenly we were no longer children. We played a lot of bridge on those rainy days. He loved to play, was always calm, infuriatingly so with his quiet 'let that go' as the ace of trumps was played. Mummy who took her card game very seriously, was irritated by this and refused to be his partner. When he and I made a Grand or Little Slam, he would shout at the top of his lungs, 'Grand Slam, Grand Slam'.

Till about 1964 he continued to go to the races. He bet some money, rarely won. When we kids attended the Gymkhana races he asked Mummy to give us some money to bet as races were no fun unless we bet money! Occasionally he would have beer, otherwise no alcohol. Once in a while he got mad about some restriction in his expenses and hollered a bit.

Through my school years, he became quite a friend. Patiently holding my poetry book in his left hand, listening carefully to check whether I was correctly reciting the poems I had learnt by heart; valiantly helping with algebra though his abilities never matched the awesome reputation Mummy claimed for him. 'He can do senior school sums by heart,' she would say in a voice filled with wonder. He would solve the problem except the answer was wrong! Next day when the teacher at school showed us how to arrive at the right answer, Papa would counter this by saying maybe methods had changed!

After his illness he was restricted to a small cash allowance. Whenever I asked him for money—to pay off a debt incurred by my fondness for sweets and *supari*—he would gladly lend me the coins. Days later, however, I would find out that everyone in the house knew I had borrowed the money from him, though I had asked that it be kept a secret. Irritated, I complained to him that it was not fair, a secret was a secret! He smiled and said nothing. He never was able to keep a secret. Once when I feared I had done badly in my annual school exams and might fail in a few subjects, I casually remarked as I left to collect the report, 'I think I'll drown myself in the sea at Haji Ali if I fail.' He replied gravely, 'No don't do that, come back home.'

I entered medical college to his great joy. Watching me read anatomy he asked me shyly, 'Do you have to read this too?' He was referring to the male sexual organs. I had a turbulent entry into the job market. I worked for barely six months as a house officer at KEM Hospital and never having had any real responsibility before, I ran headlong into problems. I got irritable on the job, fell sick and decided to quit. My professor gave up valuable hours of his time to dissuade me. Finally I withdrew my resignation and the family drew a deep breath of relief. Papa had been very concerned through all this. He had said to Mummy, 'I can't bear to see her play solitaire all day.' Later, he wanted to thank my professor for restoring my sanity! He advised me to become a super specialist, someone who was the last word on a particular subject. He said, 'Bindu, you are a good girl but you make too many enemies.' I hugged him.

He often joked how I would write his death certificate and was excited beyond belief that I was going to the USA. He called my suitcase my trousseau. Days before my scheduled departure he slipped into a coma. A week later he passed away.

Except for that last week he was never bedridden, something I'm glad fate spared him. He hated the idea of death and suspected this trip to the hospital would be his last. We discovered the day his final illness began that he was blind in one eye. He had just recovered from an ulcer in his right foot; he had been very frightened that his leg would be amputated and we had got an Xray done which showed there was no bone infection. I dressed his wound every day and thought grimly if the awful burns I dress in the hospital get better, I sure think Papa's foot should heal. By the time he had his last stroke the ulcer had gone.

It is more than twenty years since his death. Time enough for memories to settle, some distance possible, objectivity not too difficult. He was first and foremost a modern man, who had no time for ritual or religion. He was an atheist and refused to visit temples or go on pilgrimages. He was in tune with the dreams of the forward-looking of his generation. He was not politically active, lacking courage or even assertiveness against British rule. By and large he was keen to play by their rules, fit in their mould, dress as he thought his sahebs would like to see him dressed. He joined their sports club, went racing, had a box there, was about to become a steward of the Turf Club. And yet he was proud to be an Indian. He argued for and obtained the right for Indian insurers to survey and assess their marine business from Lloyds of London. In the election after 1952 he backed the Congress and Nehru. Much of his behaviour suggests rebellion, a refusal to submit to tradition and authority. His actions, however, remained isolated acts of defiance. He never sought a link with any wider movement for social change.

We never thought of his sexual needs after his stroke. Suddenly, when a friend said she had found Papa very attractive, I began to think of him as flesh and blood, as it were, not the father I knew but the man he was. He must have contained his longings in dreams of what life had been like before the stroke, only to wake up in the morning to the reality of endless celibacy. And so he lived, quietly keeping within him all the turmoil he must have felt. In many ways he was very kind, helping his siblings who had family problems. When he found Mummy crying as the financial uncertainty after his stroke was such a strain, Papa said gently, 'I can't bear to see you cry.'

I remember him today vividly, hair neatly combed into place, looking fresh after a bath and shave, crutch under his left arm, white pyjamas with elastic so that he could pull them up with one hand, a vest. He seemed content, even happy. He would read and sometimes would fall asleep on the swing. He looked forward to anyone coming, yelling 'posta' when the post came, treasuring important letters to be given to the anxious recipient with a flourish. I deprived him of a great joy towards the end of his life. He had been waiting for the permit from the USA that would allow me to work there. I found the postman at the corner of the road and took the envelope from him, smugly satisfied to have denied Papa the pleasure of shouting he had got it. He was a bit annoyed when he found I already had the letter. Why I had deliberately denied him this huge pleasure I don't know.

A few days before his final illness in 1972 an old friend came to take him for a drive. Papa's request was to go to Lamington Road, his old haunt, something his friend could not fathom and dismissed as a request too absurd to be honoured. Priti and I rode in the hearse that brought him home to Krishna Kunj from the hospital, our hands firmly holding him to keep him from slipping. Accidentally, we came via Lamington Road—we looked at each other and smiled. The last prowl, the final journey through an area where he had spent so much of himself, hurt women and maybe even hurt himself.

The swing fell from its hinges that day. The shuffle of the right foot being dragged, the open window, the familiar figure on the swing at home—gone.

Chapter Three

That Summer I was Nineteen
Iqbal Monani

A few years ago I had a letter from Choti Apa, my second sister, who lives in Karachi. Writing of our parents, she remarked, 'Do you know, we are now older than Daddy was when he died.' She is sixty-five and I am five years younger. I am not sure exactly how old Abba was when he died in 1955. He had retired prematurely from government service four years earlier when the age for retirement was fifty-five, so he must have been around fifty-seven or fifty-eight—no great age.

That summer I was nineteen, going on twenty, and preparing for the first-year law exam. One day Abba complained of a headache, brought up his lunch and had a stroke that killed him a few days later. I don't remember the exact sequence of events. I think I sat for some of the papers while he was in hospital, but I do remember the horrible feeling of insecurity his death gave me. I have a distinct memory of crying hysterically—a memory of which I have always felt rather ashamed—while his bier was being taken away, saying over and over, 'What will happen to us now?' till Apa turned on me fiercely and told me to shut up. I was the youngest of four children and not an adult in any real sense, though twenty. Perhaps, I was just a late developer, or perhaps, it was the manner in which we had been brought up, over-sheltered, cocooned and in many ways still treated as children, till death suddenly catapulted us into a harsher reality.

I have with me one of those large officially posed group photographs, taken in the early thirties, in which Abba sits surrounded by lesser officials, a charming handsome man. But I have no recollection of him as he must have looked then because we had lived away from him for six years. Starting when I was four, most of my memories of Abba are later ones when he already seemed an old man, tired and sick. Trying to recall earlier memories of him is like looking at snapshots in an album, momentary, brief and of particular incidents. One of the earliest is of his coming into the bathroom, where Mother was supervising me brushing my teeth, and telling her that war had been declared against Germany. This was in Pune, presumably in September 1939. I was a little over four then but the manner of his telling, or his tone maybe, left an impression.

This was also about the time I had been admitted into school. Another fragment of memory is of being taken to school for the first time by my father. As he turned to leave the classroom, I tried to run after him; the teacher held me back and closed the door. I think I cried and beat on the door, wanting to go out to him. My older siblings had to change schools several times on account of Abba's transfers. When Abba was informed that he was being transferred yet again, this time to Karwar on the coast of what was then called North Canara, he decided to settle the family in a rented house in Pune, where continuity of education was assured, and go off alone to his new posting.

During the time of the Second World War we lived away from Abba, visiting him twice yearly in the school vacations. Once in a while he came down on leave or on official visits, and we would see him for a few days. In those six years, the rigours of an inhospitable climate, malaria and then the scourge of diabetes aged him so much that when we rejoined him at an easier posting in 1946 he was already an old man, gaunt-faced and in poor health.

Abba must have been over thirty-five when I was born. I was the fourth and last child—almost certainly a disappointment to my parents as there were two older daughters and they had hoped for another son after my brother. Abba himself was the only surviving son of his parents, with a younger sister. My grandfather died when I was an infant. Amma, my mother, occasionally talked about him with affection. He seems to have been a rather happy-go-lucky man interested in music, poetry, gardening—all the things that don't really generate an income. My grandmother was the daughter of a minor nawab in South India. She was taciturn, practical and discouraged any show of affection or romantic feeling with scarcely veiled sarcasm. She couldn't read or write and I don't think she believed it was necessary for women to do so. Certainly she was not happy that my sisters were being sent to school. But Amma, usually so pliable, was very firm about educating us, and we were the first generation of girls in the family to be literate.

As the only son, I think my father felt his responsibilities heavily. There was some income from land but not much. Just once, remembering his childhood, my father spoke to me sadly of how he had to give up a new sherwani made for him to a visiting cousin, despite bitter tears.

Abba's early schooling was probably in Bijapur and so he spoke and wrote both Urdu and Kannada fluently, apart from English. With some assistance, very likely from his mother's side of the family, he came to Bombay and graduated from Elphinstone College, going on to take his degree in law. Those must have been hard years. However, Abba never talked to us about them except in passing. He set up practice as a lawyer, moving later into the provincial administrative services.

Some years earlier, soon after he graduated, a mutual friend had arranged his marriage to my mother. She had been orphaned as a baby and had been adopted and brought up by relations in Bombay. I don't know what my grandparents thought about a bride from the city. Why had he chosen to marry Amma? I wish I had asked Amma how it came about. Unfortunately, I never did so. My conjecture is that Abba had wanted a literate wife, someone different from the women back home. In addition it must have been reported to him that the girl proposed was pretty. Whatever the reason, he married and brought Amma back to Bijapur.

It is hard for outsiders to really understand or interpret relationships within a marriage. Close friends can, perhaps, to some degree, but a child's world begins and ends with the immediate family, and it accepts them and their interrelationships without question. My parents had been married almost ten years when I was born. I can't say other than that their's was a stable relationship, affectionate and caring, whatever the stresses. After we had grown up, Amma sometimes spoke to us with some bitterness of the early years of their marriage. She had grown up in Bombay, had gone to school for several years and was literate in three languages. She had never met my father before the wedding and like all young girls, I suppose, was hoping for a romantic husband. She began her married life in a joint family where there were many prejudices against a city-bred girl. There were often unsympathetic remarks that hurt Amma.

Having made his point by bringing home a wife of his choosing, Abba now expected her to conform to the old-fashioned ways of his parents. Strict purdah was to be observed at all times, and his mother's wishes to be respected. The closed culture of a stagnant small town must have been claustrophobic. It was hard on Amma that she did not have parents to go to for relief from this unfamiliar, limiting environment. She had to make all the adjustments.

Abba was affectionate in his way but it didn't do to make too much fuss over one's wife in a joint family. Grandmother had definite views about how much attention was to be given to wife and children. A man must pursue his work and pleasure as he saw fit. It was not manly to do otherwise. So Amma had to struggle more or less single-handedly through her pregnancies and the early years of child-rearing. Abba went regularly to the Officers'club and socialized on his own, and that was the way it was. Those years took a considerable toll on Amma's health and she always looked frail. I suppose over the years they had worked out their equation, but I think most of the giving was on Amma's side. However, Abba must have realized that she was a capable woman when he entrusted her with the task of looking after all of us and left us in Pune. With the help of live-in servants, Amma managed the household through those years quite efficiently.

When school closed we would set off to visit Abba. The train dropped us at a certain point where Abba would come to pick up his family and drive us the rest of the way. The large Chevrolet had additional folding seats at the back to accommodate all of us and little rollup blinds at the windows so that purdah could be observed. The dusty red road ran almost all the way through thick forest up and down over the mountain ridges. It followed the coastline so that sometimes the sea and the glorious unspoilt beaches came into view. At one point the car had to be ferried across as several rivers ran into the sea. Father would point out the animals and jolly us along till we arrived at the steep hill on which the official bungalow stood. The headlights would pick out the winding *kutcha* road through the darkness of a hushed forest as we swept up the final turn and crunched onto the gravel pathway and into the porch. Tired and querulous from the long drive we would be fed, washed and put to bed.

One vacation, perhaps the night we arrived, perhaps some other night, I remember waking up suddenly. There must have been a quarrel because Amma was weeping softly. Abba came into the room and picked her up and carried her away. The significance of this scene dawned on me many years later. Abba had six years of a difficult and lonely posting. Loneliness often makes strange bedfellows, and mother must have found some evidence to upset her. There were no 'scenes', nothing was ever mentioned in our hearing but with the sensitive antenna of childhood one sensed something was not quite right that holiday.

Abba took a lot of trouble to make our holidays fun. There were picnics and we went on fishing boats to the small islands that dotted the sea. Once with visiting aunts and cousins we went all the way by road to the Gersappa Falls in Mysore, where a fireworks display was put on for our benefit. I think Father enjoyed having us there as much as we looked forward to our vacations.

The area which Abba was administering was mainly forest and coastline and not much developed. Beautiful scenically, it was very cut off and the climate inhospitable. *Shikar* was the normal recreation in an area full of wildlife and he was an enthusiastic *shikari*. Tiger skins sprawled across the floors, there were smaller ones of leopards over the walls. Spotted deer skins were thrown over chairs and were used as mats on which we played. Abba was a good horseman too, but horses had made way for the automobile by this time. I do have a faint memory of Father on horseback, perhaps when I was three. Bridge and tennis were also favourite pastimes. He read whatever the Club library offered, which was mainly fiction. There were thrillers and short story collections in the house and this is when I discovered a love of books. In these years he also indulged his passion for furniture and had several good pieces made.

Abba's visits to us in Pune were exciting events. He drove down, though the distance was considerable. As we shared a compound with three other houses, his arrival was noted by our friendly neighbours. One of these had a brood of ten children and some of the younger ones were my playmates. The Chevrolet and chauffeur gave me undeserved prestige in their eyes. It also meant that we were driven to school instead of walking and the road suddenly seemed too short. I remember boasting to a classmate that Abba was in town and that he was a Collector. I was rather deflated when she asked what he collected and I was unable to explain as I didn't know what father's work was. Nobody at home really took the trouble to explain and in any case we were not encouraged to ask. This was a distinct handicap in later life.

I looked forward to Abba's visits, a little selfishly, perhaps, because he came loaded with gifts, things we had written and asked for, as well as surprises. A doll's pram with my name painted on it, a draughts board in the shape of a small table with a drawer for the pieces, were gifts I cherished for years. Often there were new clothes tailored to our approximate sizes. On one occasion father brought home red blazers for all four children. It pleased me enormously to have a garment with so many pockets.

I was a bright child and brought home good grades. Abba was full of praise and it made me proud. There was always a little cloud in the background, though. My brother, a couple of years older, hadn't settled down in school. Abba thought he was somewhat spoilt at home, being the only boy. So he arranged to admit him into a boarding school in the city. As it turned out, it was not a wise decision. My brother was very miserable, and when he came home for weekends there were copious tears and a reluctance to return to school and his grades got worse.

At about this time I must have begun to take note of intrafamily relationships. Amma, I could see, gave Abba loyalty and respect. Her voice was never raised. Her attitude filtered down to us. Abba's word was law and there was never any need for him to scold us. Abba himself showed great respect to my grandmother. When he arrived and left, he greeted her by touching her feet, a Hindu custom. Amma said this gesture was fit only for God and we were never made to imitate him. That we did not need to showed Abba respected Amma's wishes.

In most things he asked for and took her advice. Abba never called my mother by her name; and sometimes, teasingly called her Doctor. It must have been a private joke between them, the origin of which I never found out. And Amma never referred to him except as 'your father'.

Shortly after the end of the war, Abba was moved to an easier posting in Gujarat. Independence was just round the corner. Politics, however, was never mentioned in the house. It would have been indiscreet to voice opinions about the government, if one worked for the government. It was then that my eldest sister, barely seventeen and just out of school, was married off to a young lieutenant in the navy. Compared to the weddings of today it was a modest affair. I was ten and to me it seemed a fairytale wedding with *shamianas* on the tennis court and green stuff sprinkled on the ground to simulate grass. Cauldrons of food were cooked outdoors. Father's official position brought many guests besides friends and relations, as this was the first wedding in the family. The only long face at the wedding was Badi Apa's. She had not wanted to get married. She had wanted to go on to college but that was unheard of for a girl. However, things changed so fast that the very next year when Choti Apa matriculated and we came to live with Father, it became perfectly possible for her to join the local college! Perhaps the fact that my grandmother had passed away in the year between had something to do with it.

After many years of seeing Abba off and on, we rejoined him in 1946. Independence came in 1947 and the Union Jack which used to flutter outside the official bungalow gave place to the Tricolour. These must have been stressful times for Abba with all the communal flare-ups following the partition of the country. He had opted to remain in India. There was no doubt in his mind that he belonged here. It came as a shock to him that his son-in-law, without consulting him or his own father, had opted for Pakistan.

Whatever the strain on Abba, we lived a normal existence through those two years. Once or twice we were allowed to accompany him on his official tours. I still remember the joy of living under canvas and coming out early in the morning to the freshness of dew-spangled grass and the smell of wood smoke. On one occasion we went on a crocodile shoot. During one of these tours Abba picked up an infection and was ill with a violent attack of jaundice. As allopathy had nothing in the way of a cure, I remember the local hakim saheb clipclopping up to the house in a horse carriage to treat him. About this time the diabetes was also diagnosed. From then on I think father's health began to go downhill.

It was while we were in Gujarat that I also had my first confrontation, if it can be called that, with Abba. I wanted a pet and nobody would get me one. We already had several dogs, a horse, a buffalo, a goat or two and a run of chickens. But I wanted a pet of my very own. So when a classmate mentioned that her cat had littered, I went off after school to get myself a kitten, without telling anybody. The servant who collected my brother and me from school in a tonga couldn't find me, and when I did rejoin them on their way home it was late and everyone at home had got very anxious. Father was furious when he learnt why we had been delayed, and I was subjected to his temper for perhaps the first time in my life. Father never raised his hand against us but his stern glare with flaring nostrils was enough to quell us. This time he was really angry and thundered, 'Drown that cat'. As we lived on the banks of the Tapi River this prospect made me burst into tears. Fortunately, Mother came to the rescue and I was allowed to keep the kitten.

Soon after, Abba was transferred to Bombay and we followed when the school term was over. Used to an independent style of functioning, he found the secretariat uncongenial and decided to retire prematurely. He did not want to remain in Bombay as he didn't like large cities. However, except for my eldest sister none of the three children was settled, we had not even completed our education. There was little choice, and we remained in Bombay, in a house my mother had inherited and which Abba had extended.

Used to large official houses and plenty of garden space, Abba felt cramped living in a house that opened straight onto the street. It was noisy and the upstairs-downstairs arrangement, uncomfortable. With little to do, he took to attending auctions and sales.

Already the house was cluttered with furniture—one of Abba's joys—despite a lot having been sold off when we moved. Now, to Mother's despair, we acquired more, some of it quite unsuitable; large second-hand carpets with the moth already in them and roll-top tables that were showing signs of woodworm.

Physically unwell, Abba let himself go. He had to monitor his blood sugar and take his daily shot of insulin himself. Often unshaved and refusing to wear his dentures, he looked much older than his years. With the fastidiousness of adolescence I found this embarrassing when my friends dropped in. Sometimes in the middle of a meal, finding his dentures uncomfortable, Father would remove them and hand them to me to put away. Seeing the look of horror on my face, Amma would chide him gently. I think our image of Abba—mine as well as my siblings'—changed at this point. He was no longer the strong, reassuring figure he had been to us before. In close proximity we saw him differently and sometimes his ideas and ours clashed.

Our lifestyle had naturally changed. We were no longer chauffeured everywhere. Abba couldn't keep track of all our activities and this probably worried him. One evening when Choti Apa, who was now at medical college, failed to come home at the usual hour, he collared me to go with him and look for her. She was in none of the places we went to. It was past 9 p.m. by the time she got back. On being told about our going to look for her, she flew at him—why did he have to embarrass her before her friends? Was she not grown up enough to go to a film show with her friends sometimes? As there was no telephone in the house how could she have let us know? Quite taken aback, Abba conceded the point without more ado.

I was a more docile child but even I showed my resentment when Abba opened a letter addressed to me. I think these outbursts from us baffled him a little. He complained to Amma, who pointed out that we were growing up and times were changing. It made him feel he was getting old and this worried him too because he could see that it was going to be some years before any of us would be in a position to earn a living.

Money was becoming a problem. He had not been able to save much and inflation was beginning to increase day-to-day expenses. Both Amma and he had heavy medical expenses. To augment his pension Father decided to build a couple of small houses in Bijapur for rent. The land was already there. Abba went off to Bijapur with our old cook to look after him. I have a strange recurring dream about Abba which probably stems from these times. In the dream I have this peculiar anxiety about him being away. I am not sure whether he is dead or will return. Sometimes he does return and then I do not know how to deal with him because he is no longer a part of my life. So much has changed while he has been away. I think his being unwell and his going away must have made me very anxious even at the time, though I was not aware of it or did not want to admit it to myself. I was just beginning to realize that there were difficulties about money. For the first time there were arguments, mild but worrying, about the daily expenses. We couldn't afford this or that. Abba complained about his medical bills. He practiced little economies himself, such as walking instead of using the car. He had stopped driving as his eyesight had worsened. We couldn't afford a full-time driver. Unspoken anxieties, perhaps, found a permanent lodging somewhere in my subconscious. I was too young to be consulted about problems but not too young to realize that these existed.

Abba was still in Bijapur when my brother and I finished our school finals. Amma decided we should spend our vacations with him. As it turned out, it was not a happy time for me, Living with my father at the time was a Shah Saheb, one of the wolves-in-saints' garb, whom my parents, particularly my mother, fell prey to from time to time,. The wretched man made advances to me and I was too embarrassed to tell Abba. Sometimes I wonder how Abba never noticed. I was not yet fifteen and spent the vacation in a turmoil of distress.

While we were in Bijapur our examination results appeared in the *Times of India*. Not so many students sat for the examinations in those days. I had done fairly well; my brother had flunked, for the second time. I was sad, not so much for my brother as for Abba. I could see the distress it caused him. Over the years I had seen his growing anxiety for my brother. He never scolded him, whereas Amma did, often. He merely arranged for more tuitions and spoke to Amma of his anxiety.

Abba was keen that I join Elphinstone College. It was his old alma mater. I would have preferred to join Wilson College with some of my friends; it was just round the corner from where we lived. However, I gave in, and never regretted it. Elphinstone was still a well-run, prestigious institution in the fifties, one of the best, with distinguished alumni. Another happy outcome was my getting to know my husband there. He was a year my senior and a very visible student. We met again years later and married.

Abba returned from Bijapur with the additional complication of virulent sinusitis. The dust and the heat had aggravated an existing weakness and nothing seemed to help the condition which was not a pleasant one. Diabetes limited his diet in one way and high blood pressure in another. It was distressing to see him so unwell. At the same time his hopes that incoming rent from the houses he had built would ease financial strain were not realized. Trying to work on his own he had miscalculated and the post often brought in several outstanding bills for building materials. Bijapur was a small place and rents were low. He decided to have a young couple occupy the first floor of our house as paying guests. Just then the administrative services were expanding, and this was a period of acute shortage of accommodation in Bombay. The government requisitioned the flat. Abba went to court and after two years of litigation was able to regain possession. The strain of all this told on his already weakened health.

Most of Abba's interests required physical fitness and he was now in no condition to pursue any of them. He remained more and more at home. He enjoyed seeing an occasional film. I remember one film to which he and I went one afternoon, unusual because it was just the two of us. I remember that we didn't take a taxi; we walked and all the way I was worrying that he might stumble. I had joined the women's hockey team at college and sometimes stayed on to practice. Abba would be waiting on the balcony for my return. I used to think it rather tiresome of him. Looking back, I think it probably was also a way for him to pass the time, watching all the activity in the street below. He often lay in bed listening to Indian classical music on the radio. Philistines that we were, we would ask if we could tune in to the film songs relayed on Radio Ceylon. I still remember the smile with which he nodded assent. He enjoyed reading P. G. Wodehouse and so did I, but we never discussed the books. I don't remember discussing anything with Abba. I suppose the habit of communication has to be cultivated, even between parents and children, perhaps with more effort, I think. He was not a very articulate person, or perhaps it was his upbringing that made him so. However, that he was very fond of me communicated itself; also that my small academic achievements were something he was proud of.

One of my saddest memories of this time is of Abba coming home with a newspaper and asking me to check again if my brother's number was among the successful candidates in the Inter-Science examination. It was not. Wearily and very sadly Abba merely said, 'Don't tell him yet. It will upset him.' I remember feeling very angry with my brother, knowing how much his repeated failures worried Abba. It was some compensation that his daughters were doing well, but he couldn't see what his son's future was going to be.

When I graduated Abba wanted me to go on to law college. It was not a good assessment of my abilities. I was shy and tonguetied when it came to mixing with people or expressing an opinion. I lacked confidence and was not really mature even for my age. Partly, I suppose, it was my own temperament, partly it was because we were actively discouraged from mixing with people outside or thinking for ourselves. Abba himself was not a gregarious man. Amma had a circle of relations and any socializing was only within that circle. Attempts to have close friends were frowned upon. We were the first generation of girls to be educated and out of purdah. There must have been a constant struggle in our parents' minds about how much freedom we were to have, and they erred on the side of prudence. I was not likely material for the legal battlefield but joined the law college anyway. I remember very little of my two years there, continuing for one more year after Abba's death, abandoning law for ever when a job on a small literary magazine was offered to me. It suited my introvert personality much more and was a source of steady income, small though it was.

When I look around me today and see with what panache young women now enter varied and interesting careers I wonder why I did not make better use of the opportunities I was given. Firstly, perhaps I did not realize they were opportunities. I took them for granted. It was only many years after Abba died and I went to Bijapur on some work that I suddenly realized what these opportunities were. I met women who were uneducated and in strict purdah. They gave a curious impression of childishness and stupidity and I was horrified to think I could have been like them. It was difficult to find any topics of conversation. Mercifully, a manservant's voice calling '*ghosha ghosha*' (a warning to remain unseen) sent them scattering into inner rooms and I took my leave. I am talking of over twenty-five years ago and I do hope things have changed for the younger generation there, as they had for us so much earlier, thanks to our parents. Because Amma with stubborn courage insisted that her daughters must go to school, the door to progress was opened to us. For this I am immensely grateful to her and to Father who went along with her ideas.

Secondly, possibly not as many fields were open to anyone, men or women, in a world just recovering from the trauma of a long and ghastly war. Thirdly, there was a peculiar ambivalence in the manner of our upbringing, and it has always troubled me. I do not hold this against my parents. The pace of change had accelerated so suddenly that they couldn't be comfortable with it. Today I find the same difficulty with my daughters. I want them to have all the freedom possible to fulfill themselves and be part of their times, yet I am afraid for them because the values prevailing now are not ours, and strike me as not quite right. I suppose, just like we try to, our parents did the best they could. Their ambivalence lay in wanting education for us and in wanting us nonetheless to conform to old patterns of thought and behaviour.

Long before I grew up my gender role was, so to say, defined for me. I still remember vividly the bewilderment with which I had heard the laughter of Abba and some other adults when, not to be left out, I had asserted that like my brother I would be a judge when I grew up. I must have been five or so at that time. Over and over I remember when I was very young being restrained from interesting physical activities like horse riding, swimming, cycling because they were not for girls. On the other hand efforts to sew, or embroider or cook were praised. I was often scolded for trying to follow my brother around when he was with his friends. The message that came across was that the world outside the home was the men's domain. They were privileged and superior beings. And yet a good school report was praised. The highest praise that one was given was: 'It's a pity you are not a boy.' Later the necessity arose to compete with men at university and in a career. By that time the earlier messages had been so internalized, it was hard to change. I never felt comfortable with the other sex. I had been made too aware of their differences sexually. This and a lack of confidence prevented me from even trying to spread my wings. Rebellion came much later, but tempered by good sense so that no harm came of it finally.

It is almost forty years since my Abba passed away. I think back to his many wordless gestures that spelt affection, care and pride. Had he lived longer we might have clashed, but as it happened I can only remember him with love and some sadness.

Chapter Four

Out of the Top Drawer
Jane Pillai

When I think of my father, his tall lean frame, large capable hands with bony wrists, pale blue eyes with unruly eyebrows, shaggy moustache, upright way of standing, all come to mind. When he walked into a room everyone, not only I, was aware of his presence. In his youth he had been immaculately dressed by tailors in London, his shoes hand-stitched to fit the elegant wooden and brass shoe-trees that were made to measure to fit his feet. Even when I knew him best the bearing was the same, the shoes were polished like chestnuts even if the jacket was old and shabby, and the pullover, worn defiantly, full of holes that he refused to allow to be darned. As a child I would walk up his long legs, my hands securely held until I reached his waist. Then he would swing me onto his shoulders. I knew the feeling of his frame and the texture of his jackets long before we were able to communicate in other terms. I learnt that his moustache tickled when he kissed me and that his strong hands were calloused and rough, but however shabby the outer layer, there was always a smell of eau de cologne, soap and hair oil, and his handkerchief was of cool linen or silk. His chest of drawers had the same fragrance, the drawers kept very tidy, his holey pullovers neatly folded, while the top drawer contained, as he put it, his treasures.

His monogrammed silver-backed brushes stood on a yellow glass tray, and all his life he liked to shave using a leather strop and a murderous cut-throat razor. I loved to watch him shaving in the morning with his leather braces hanging over his hips, and the lather hiding most of his face. He would make faces at me in the mirror as he wielded his razor like a conductor's baton. He always treated me with extreme courtesy, even when I was very small, and would ceremoniously escort me down to breakfast, calling me Missy, so that I felt different from my brothers and sorry that the royal familiarity was for me alone. With my brothers his tone was different, perhaps he was not aware of it, but it was demeaning and painful when he referred to them as Old Man, Old Cockerlaurum, or Juggins instead of by their names. This usually accompanied a reprimand or a correction and placed an uncrossable distance between them.

Towards our mother, his tone was both authoritative and appreciative but not familiar, and it was only much later in their lives that I felt that they could communicate in public on the same level. At table, the conversation was generally subdued, and it was only when he left the room that we could talk freely and laugh and make jokes with our mother. I know now that this was due to his Victorian upbringing and probably he was almost an adult before he was allowed to sit down to meals with his parents. Our mother had also been brought up with a strict Victorian grandmother but had been surrounded by warmth, besides which she was an American, so she could laugh and make us laugh, and gently break the code of etiquette into more human terms.

Although we never heard so from my father's lips, we slowly guessed that his own childhood had not always been a happy one. The eldest of five children, my father did tell us that he had organized their escape from a convent when they were all too young to have been sent away from home. He thought it amusing that the nuns overhearing his plans had offered to pack sandwiches for their long walk home. We found this sad, not funny, and later we discovered that his mother had slipped into alcoholism, and although she doted on my father, she created unhappiness by pitting one child against another. One glimpsed the chilly disciplines of an Edwardian childhood, the nursery, the bread and butter puddings, the isolation of children from their parents.

I think mother was largely responsible for making us understand that such an upbringing had contributed to our father's reserve and unapproachability and that we must be careful not to upset him. She built in us a sense of loyalty and tried her best to make the atmosphere cheerful and kept us from provoking arguments which would lead to days of silent coldness on my father's part. Later when financial problems became stressful, she never criticized or humiliated him but tried to solve them in practical ways. It was her patience and understanding and sense of fun that transformed him from a difficult young man into the father that we knew. Mother had a kind of loyalty and sweetness which is rare today, and belonged to a gentler, older, code of ethics.

My father never lost his military bearing, but his army career was very brief, and I believe that his experience as a young boy of eighteen in the First World War marked him for life. He rarely spoke about it, but his horror of physical suffering and bloodshed was so acute that he must have been profoundly shocked by this exposure at such a young age. When his colonel and company commander were killed, he led the abandoned company into an attack. Mentioned in dispatches (the reports sent from the scene of battle to the government in London, singling out special examples of bravery), he was made an honorary captain and after the war was asked to carry the Regimental Colours at a Victory parade in Cardiff, when he was presented to the Prince of Wales. He had an aversion for the smell of blood and warned by our mother, we hid the more gory of our wounds from him. We also kept it secret that he once went to donate blood and fainted and had to be brought home. I do not think that his family's pride in his success eradicated his horror, and as his lungs were also damaged by poison gas, his father sent him to work on a cargo boat for healing doses of sea air. Many years later I came across his seaman's pass granting him permission to embark at San Diego at the age of twenty.

When his lungs cleared, he went to the University of Oxford. Not really interested in an intellectual career, he then joined the family business in Cardiff and no doubt his father wished that he should succeed him and also that he should make a suitable marriage to cement his position in society. I know that he was not a puritan, that he had an eye for pretty women and that he loved to dance but he was aware that his family was regarded as social upstarts. When a girl at a large country house sniggered at his gold watch chain, he was sensitive enough to realize that his looks and wealth were not enough in the savage snobbery of those days.

He saw my mother on a transatlantic liner when she was returning with her family from a tour of Europe and he was bound for America on a business trip. He remarked to his friend that he had just seen the person he would like to marry. Under her mother's apprehensive eyes he paid her a good deal of attention, borrowing a book from her so that he could trace her in America. They were married before his tour ended, and he returned in triumph with her to his family in Cardiff.

I can understand how she must have felt like a lamb thrown to the lions. She was too pretty and gentle with a translucent skin, dark auburn hair and deep blue eyes. Although my grandfather approved of her, my grandmother was moody, unpredictable and cold. Her brothers-and sisters-in-law, eyed her with reservation, commenting behind her back on her style, and her accent while taking into account her gentle defenceless manner. My father was proud of her but he puzzled her with his long silences and by contradicting her often at dinner parties if she laughed too much or paid too much attention to their guests. She eased her sense of foreignness by transforming his home. Denied pets in her youth, she now kept a succession of dogs, cats, chicks, goslings and, once, a goat. My father learnt to laugh with her at their antics, gradually breaking down his shyness and reserve.

It became almost a cruel joke in my father's family that they were anxious to have children, but the years passed with a series of miscarriages and disappointments. After eight years, they decided to adopt a family, and their first child was my elder brother, Peter. Blond, blue-eyed, and high spirited, he became the central focus of my mother's life. Three years later, I was brought home, the year before the Second World War destroyed their way of life.

The prospect of war and the certainty that the steel industry would be nationalized made Grandfather advise his sons to opt out of the family concern. My father bought a farm in the depths of Somerset, a few miles away from the nearest village and under the looming side of the moors with a bus that ran once a week to Minehead. It was in complete contrast to the sophisticated life that my parents had lived before. Cardiff and Bristol had become targets of German bombardments and my earliest memories are of wailing sirens followed by terrifying bangs before we moved to the peace and sanity of a tiny cottage up on Exmoor while the farm was being renovated. My mother was appalled by the isolation and the magnitude of running a farm practically single-handed. My father, never very communicative, now had no time for anything but his dairy herd, a flock of sheep, rotating crops. He slept out in a shepherd's hut at lambing time, dealt with ploughing and harvesting, and a photograph of him at this time shows him with a tense lined face as if the time spared to pose for it were ill-afforded.

Once we were settled on the farm, our youngest brother arrived and we took it for granted that all babies came from London complete with leggings and feeding bottles. Although our father lived with us we rarely saw him, and he was so physically tired that at mealtimes our mother tried to keep us as quiet as possible. As an outsider, my mother always made us see things from a distance so that I never really understood our social niche, which even in the postwar days had clearly demarcated boundaries. That we were kept apart from the village children because we were gentlefolk did not fit in with our father working with his own hands to put our large house into order. That he was living on his capital and laboured manually in the garden to grow food for us, put us outside of normal categories and as I grew I longed for a sure social identity which would link us with other children and not make us feel isolated.

At this stage in our lives our father had changed from being the eldest son and heir in a wealthy industrial family in Wales with everything given to him by his ambitious father: schooling at Shrewsbury (a well-known public school), a career in the Welsh Guards (a prestigious regiment), a seat at Oxford, a place at the helm of the family business, a flat in Jermyn St (an aristocratic address), a life membership of a London club, wealth and opportunity that made his younger brothers envious of him. He put it all behind him, choosing to run a farm during the war years and finally relinquishing all these to care for us when the war ended.

It was some time then that my eldest brother was sent away to boarding school. After a brief spell in the local village school, a visiting school inspector discovered that my constant stomach ache was due to tuberculosis, and I was sent away for a year to a special hospital in Hampshire. Cut off from the family, I found it strange and upsetting that during my absence the farm had been sold. My youngest brother and I were sent to stay with an uncle. Peter had developed severe asthma attacks. My mother was in a nursing home in Hereford and my father decided to turn his attention to his ailing family.

A Victorian dower house (a small house on a large country estate) in my uncle's village had been lying unoccupied for eleven years, so my father bought it and installed us in a home that took its lighting from an eccentric generator in a shed and heated its bath water with a malevolent, ill-tempered stove. He put his heart and mind into restoring the house and nursing his family back to health, caring not a bit that his clothes were covered with splashes of paint or that he wheeled barrows of manure into the vegetable garden. It was now that all three of us children came into close contact with him and slowly made his real acquaintance. We had to get used to seeing a great deal of him every day. He still seemed rather unapproachable, a tall man with stern blue eyes and sometimes a set, unsmiling mouth. We would become uncertain in front of him, and he felt too unsure of us to make the first move.

The winter of 1947 was famous for its severity and our village was cut off by deep snow drifts from the railway station and the main road. My mother was stranded in her nursing home in Hereford, and we were alone in the large empty house with my father. It must have been very hard for him. In the evenings, he did what he never had done before: he read to us. The book was *The Wind in the Willows* and I always associate its beautiful language with the sound of his voice. I slowly learnt to lean against him, comforted by the rough tweed beneath my cheek or fingertips. Once he was taking me upstairs by the hand when the awful emptiness of the house overcame me and I sobbed. He asked me if I was missing our mother and when I nodded he replied that he was too, which made me see him as a different person. He tried to do all that our mother did for us, laying out our morning clothes with military precision and I felt too scared to point out that he had mixed up our socks. He cooked nursery meals of prunes and rice puddings to be eaten without a murmur, and we were all relieved when our mother came home at last. It was during this period that I had the worst nightmares I have ever experienced. I would wake up in the night in a sweat of terror, and when my parents answered my frantic calls, it was not my mother's hand or voice that calmed me but my father's handkerchief, smelling of cologne, tucked under my cheek that made the terror recede into the shadows of the room.

As we grew older we became aware that he was pained by our familiarity and close proximity to our mother. She was ready at all times to listen to us, a cat on her lap, a dog near her feet, all of us teasing her and she teasing us back. When my father walked in, a silence would fall and he would inevitably say that it was time for a meal or time for us to go to bed as if he wanted to separate us from her and have her exclusively for himself. There was always a pang of guilt that we were keeping her from him. When at last he did begin to laugh at our jokes, and even make a few of his own, we all felt an individual sense of triumph and relief that he had joined us at last and was no longer an exile.

When my younger brother and I first went to school, my father had to drive us there as it was some distance away. Once we stopped to give a tramp a lift; he got in the front beside my father and turning around wished us good morning in an educated voice. I think we were too surprised by his squalor to reply. After he had thanked my father and got down, we drove on for a while. Suddenly, my father braked the car and turned on us in anger. At his most cold and stern he told us never to be rude again by staring, and that we should have wished good morning first because the man was dirty and poor. He was genuinely angry and when I considered it, as I often did, I realized that he was not just angry with us but at a world which allowed such things to exist. Never a snobbish man, he cared for those whom he felt to be on a different social level. I saw that amongst the people who lived in our village he was held in as much respect as he held them. No one presumed to call him by his first name, although his lifestyle matched theirs. He was always Mr. Alan.

In his political views he was a conservative, a man of habit, who made no mental effort to question too deeply the social mores of English country life. Neither did he agree with nor did he fit into the pattern of feeling himself in any way superior to the simple labourers in the village. With them he was simply himself. Amongst the people with whom my mother wished to be friendly, he was considered to be eccentric and odd, and he could be surprisingly rude if he felt people of his own social standing were being shallow or frivolous, which made the rare social events a strain for us all. He had an embarrassing antipathy towards vicars and we were often unsure of what he might say. When he arrived for my younger brother's christening service in his gumboots my mother was reduced to tears of mortification. Amongst my mother's closest friends few understood him, or forgave his social blunders, and this made me sympathize with him as I always felt upset that they had not taken the trouble to understand him. I know this awkward behaviour made my brothers very cautious in their dealings with him, and I was aware of my mother's constant efforts to keep him calm and happy, and the family at peace.

My mother liked to go to country furniture sales and often returned with treasures, one of which was an old croquet set, and my father taught us to play. The sound of mallet and ball combined with the smell of mown grass and honeysuckle conjures up home and happiness. In the winter evenings he decided to teach us all to play canasta, a forerunner to bridge if we were intelligent he said, although he never otherwise played cards himself. But he joined us in noisy games where cheating was allowed and for the first time the reserve that was between us all was banished.

He taught us never to be ashamed of our bodies; when small we were encouraged to have water fights on the lawn on warm summer afternoons, my brothers and I running around naked and quite unselfconscious. He never locked bathroom doors or expected them to be locked, welcoming any of us in for a chat as he lay in his bath, sometimes asking us to sponge his back. This profoundly shocked some of my parents' friends but I think it took away curiosity and fear. Later on in our teens, we barricaded ourselves in but initially there was no prudery or shyness. I saw my body as a natural phenomenon, part of the process of life as I had seen the birthing of lambs and kittens. From a very early age, we had been told that we had not actually come from our mother's body but were specially chosen, and we accepted this as a comforting alternative. It was not until we had left home and saw ourselves against others that the painful self-questioning set in.

My father bought an ancient caravan, shaped like an egg, made out of wood and canvas, probably a collector's item, to be towed by a car. He taught us to write up a log book and gave us all assignments that lent an excitement and imaginative content to the most simple events. The important thing we learnt was never to question its destination or his choice, as we did not want any unhappy silences to fall, and because my mother acquiesced with good grace, she taught us the art not merely of submission but of seeing another person's delight blossom.

We were banished to boarding school that year. Ejected suddenly from the privacy and familiarity of home, and set amidst many girls of my own age made me very homesick, unsure of myself, with a misery that seemed to last for years. It was at this period that I wished my parents were like others, that we lived in suburbia, that my father worked in a bank, that my mother was English and most of all that my father would be appropriately dressed on Parents' Day. As I left childhood and entered into my teens, I could not imagine what I should aim for afterwards. A schism developed between school and home that made me feel I was two different people but my father remained unperturbed and unaware that life was changing under my feet.

After he sold the farm, my father had been living on his capital;

boarding school for three children meant an increasing strain. I began to be acutely aware of my mother's anxiety about financial matters. On the surface my father seemed blithely unaware, refusing to listen to anyone's advice and trusting his bank manager to do the needful, but eventually he had to look for a job in the nearest town. He became a partner in a brush factory but he disliked it intensely and so asked an old colleague in the Steel Company of Wales if he could suggest something better. He was offered a job in the small tin-plating works at Lydney, which had been designed by his own father, and had circumstances been different might now have been his.

So my father gave up the peace of his garden and returned to the setting in which he had grown up, only now he was in a position of lesser privilege. It did not seem to worry him. What concerned him was the discovery of dishonesty in the management, but when he reported this he was told that if he wished to keep his place he must remain silent. He began to have a series of terrible headaches, sitting quietly in his chair, silent again, while my mother frantically thought of ways to help him. It was apparent that the upkeep of the large house and garden was becoming too difficult. After two years away in Germany, my eldest brother had married and left home. My younger brother and I at university and art college were both too preoccupied to be of any help. A friend from his Oxford days offered him a job in the Midlands and reluctantly my parents decided to sell the home. I still dream of its individual rooms with their sounds and fragrances. Perhaps that is the price of happiness.

We moved to a small village in Northamptonshire that consisted of one main street, a stream, a cascading cluster of chestnut trees and ancient thatched cottages. Although it was a pretty place, there was something closed and static about its atmosphere. It was one of several villages belonging to the Duke of Buccleuch, for whom my father now worked, running a poultry farm on an aerodrome that had been abandoned by the Americans after the war. My father was quite content to do this as he understood livestock, but again in that small community we belonged to no fixed group and remained outsiders, as most of the villagers had lived there all their lives and accepted the rigid social hierarchy.

At this stage, I was a postgraduate student at the Royal College of Art in London and the division between college and home was as severe as it ever had been. There was a transition from rural quiet to an atmosphere not only of an aggressive professionalism but of values and attitudes that were alien to me. Almost all the students who were with me were from a different social background, and many such as David Hockney seemed to know how to operate in a competitive urban society. It was a London coming back to life after the postwar gloom, the Swinging Sixties, with a reshuffling of society; my contemporaries on the whole, seemed much more worldly-wise than I. It seemed to mock my ineptitude and soft middle-class background and a curious unreality seemed to pervade everything. I never thought of telling my parents about it and tried to be as I always had been, happy to be home, but a sense of restriction set in and sometimes I caught my father watching me intently when he thought I was not looking. He arranged that I could use the old village schoolroom as a studio and I spent many hours painting there in the large room with a cast iron stove and tall church windows.

During a summer exhibition of our paintings at the Royal College my tutor's son, Michael Buhler, came up to me and said I looked so out of place. He asked if my father was a stockbroker or an established businessman in the City, the business district of London. It touched a very sensitive spot, as I did not know my feelings or appearance were so obviously different. A mental picture arose of my father riding his bicycle down the village street, his trouser bottoms tied with string, an ancient Panama hat on his head which he would raise to young mothers hanging out their washing in their gardens or to the elderly ladies lifting white lace curtains to watch him go by. He, however, was perfectly happy and always himself and saw no reason for anyone to be otherwise.

As my time at the Royal College was coming to an end, I realized that my parents' attention was becoming focussed on my future. Did I betray their kindness and trust by deciding to look for a job in India, feeling that I had to leave home so that I could see myself alone, unreflected in their mirror? If they were apprehensive, they hid their feelings from me while I wrote many letters to any school or college in India whose address I came across. If I had chosen America instead, they would have had the reassurance of family ties and familiar terrain. But I deliberately chose to be alone to see if I could survive unaided in totally strange surroundings, away from rural passivity or the awkward politics of a more public artistic life. I left for India with a return ticket in my possession, assuring them that my absence was only for one year.

India was more beautiful than I had anticipated and when one is alone, the sights and sounds are more clearly seen. During the year that I spent in India I wrote many letters home, and my father carefully filed them all. During my absence my young cousin Dee came to visit my parents and her concern and affection for them filled the void which I had left. I felt relieved when my mother wrote happily of her visits. My contract with the school had practically finished when I received an anguished telegram from my father saying that my mother had suffered a severe heart attack. Desolated, I flew home as soon as I could, feeling very unwell myself. Luckily a doctor in London identified jaundice before I had taken the infection home. My homecoming was a blur in a hospital ward but my mother wrote a cheerful letter to me and sent me a yellow bedjacket to match my eyes. When I finally reached home she seemed better than I had anticipated, and my father hovered anxiously around us both. He took over most of the responsibilities of running the house until he was convinced we had both rested enough.

I did not know how to tell him about Sushil whom I had met a short while before leaving India and who seemed more familiar to me than anyone I had ever met. Our earliest conversation had been about our families, and when he heard of my mother's illness he sent her a Naga shawl that he had collected while working in Nagaland. She wrote to thank him for it and wore it draped over her knees when we sat recuperating under the apple trees. That autumn I was offered a job in the painting department at the Liverpool College of Art, and I was able to come home at frequent intervals. Outwardly, my mother seemed to return to her former self, but she lay longer in bed surrounded by gardening books and catalogues, making plans for the seasons ahead. My father willingly planted everything that she ordered, and she was soon out in the garden again. She hid from us that her lungs were troubling her so that my father and I shut out from our minds the possibility that she might suffer a relapse.

My parents never told me that they were fully aware of the number of letters that I wrote to India or that they heard me going downstairs as soon as I heard the postman bang the gate. Of their pillow talks and anxieties, I knew nothing until I read my mother's diaries after her death.

After two years, when my mother's condition appeared to have stabilized, Sushil wrote and said would I, despite all foreseeable problems agree to marry him and return to Delhi where he had been posted. Letters were written from my parents to his mother, and as I prepared to leave Liverpool and my home I could not let myself think that anything could happen to my mother, and they never so much as hinted that I should not go.

I flew to Delhi where official permission was needed from Army Headquarters before we could be married. Since I was a foreigner, my parents stipulated that I should find a job and be self-sufficient until I had the opportunity to meet Sushil's family. After visiting many of the schools I finally found a vacancy, but on the day that my letter of appointment came, the most terrible telegram arrived from my father informing me that my mother had died that morning. There was no question of my staying, and I flew back to England on the next available flight. It was wrenching to see my father's agony, and I had no time to let the grief in my own heart melt. My mother had wished to be cremated and because she had always felt a stranger in England, she did not want a headstone to mark her final resting place. She had requested that her ashes should be scattered in the garden they had made together. The local vicar reluctantly agreed to read the burial service in the garden and my father excluded everyone except my brothers and their wives and myself. Bereft of ceremony and ritual, we all seemed so utterly alone, the words soon over and the ashes inexpertly scattered and visible under the Michaelmas daisies and miniature shrubs of the herbaceous border.

When my brothers left, I was alone to witness the most agonizing grief I have ever seen. My father who always seemed so strong seemed to fold and crumple in his misery, the tears wrenched and wracked, and I did not know how to stem their desperate flow. It never occurred to me to contact a doctor; he had excluded relatives, and without anyone to advise me I could only let him sob. Fearing that he would harm himself I once begged him to stop. He asked me my age and when I told him, he said that I could not comprehend what it was like to have a companion for forty years and to lose her in a matter of minutes. I knew he was right and I hung over the wooden fence that divided our garden from the farmer's field, feeling inadequate to ease his pain.

I spent several months with my father, and gradually his anguish quietened as he slowly came to terms with his grief. For the first time he began to attend church services, saying that he could best think of my mother there. He wanted nothing of hers touched or removed and yet the sight of her belongings would cause fresh tears to flow. I slowly packed away her things. I think the most generous gesture that he ever made to me was to encourage me to return to India to marry Sushil, trusting in my choice. I did not want to leave him but he kept insisting that I should. I returned to Delhi in a kind of daze and we were married soon after.

In our first period of leave we flew to England and spent a month there with my father. He was much calmer and had made a programme for Sushil to meet as many members of the family as possible. When my father and Sushil stood next to each other I saw that they were of identical shape and in many ways had the same sensibilities. I hope that my father felt the same way, that my choice was to continue to be with someone like him and not a radical departure. I felt as if I were passing so effortlessly from one life into the next, but I also realized the cost to my father by this severance.

I did not want to leave my father alone again, but he insisted on his independence, and although Peter offered to share a home with him in Cardiff, he said that he wished to remain in the cottage for some more time. Nevertheless, it came as a painful shock when he wrote to me a few months later asking my permission to marry Dee's mother, his youngest brother's widow, whom I had not seen for many years. He had written a similar letter to both my brothers. For the first time in our lives it was a reversal of roles, and we realized that our opinions really mattered to him. We wrote and wished him happiness and he was married in the autumn of that year, a little over a year after my mother's death.

It was then that my own private dam of tears burst as if they had no end. I was shocked at the feelings that arose of surprise, loss and betrayal, and in some way I knew that I was responsible. My mother's brother wrote a very comforting letter to me from Los Angeles, saying that he understood perfectly well why my father had remarried so soon and that I must try and understand as well.

Before Sushil and I had left England I had requested my father to write to me as often as he could and he had promised that he would. Every day in the evening until he was eighty years old, he kept his promise. Retreating to his small desk with a glass of sherry at hand, he would write a few lines in the form of a diary, describing his daily activities, a description of the weather, or that the wild ducks had returned to the stream, and although he never wrote about his feelings, I could deduce that he was all right and had thought of me before my aunt called him down to supper. Because my father wanted nothing changed in the cottage and was not prepared to move, it became more difficult for my aunt to stay. Homesick for her own daughters and friends in Devon, they mutually agreed to live in their own houses, commuting between the two, but it defeated the purpose of marriage and meant long stretches of time alone.

When my father was seventy-three he came to visit us in India for the first time. Although my friends had warned me that the journey might be too much for him, he came jauntily off the plane, waving a mop that I had asked him to bring. He was excited and happy. I was apprehensive that the chaotic drive from Delhi to Dehra Dun would exhaust him, but he remained interested and alert all the way. He made it clear that he just wanted to be at home with us and to share our lives and did not expect to be taken to the usual tourist attractions. The Indian Military Academy interested him a great deal and he liked to see the cadets. He would take longs walks on his own, looking at everything. He was fascinated to discover mules, something he had not seen since 1918, and he liked to practice golf on the empty course in the morning, more interested in the monkeys in the trees and the crow that flew away with his golf ball. I was teaching and so he was alone for half the day but it was always as if he had brought his own private world with him to our back verandah, and I would return to the smell of Rich Dark Honeydew tobacco and find him sitting quietly, our puppy at his feet, gazing at the Mussoorie hills or at the parrots' noisy ravaging of the lichi trees.

He thought India beautiful and when I asked him if he found anything upsetting he replied that, on the contrary, he had been so interested to see so many different people all getting on with their own lives. We went for many picnics into the forests around Dehra Dun, but I particularly remember one day at Rishikesh when he sat on a large rock, his trouser bottoms rolled up so that he could dabble his feet in the water, as he gazed at the jade green Ganges, lost in his own thoughts. For once, the bridge between my various lives was perfectly in place.

Five years later I took our small daughter to see him in England, as I knew I could not ask him to undertake such a long journey again. When I saw him I realized sadly how age had caught up with him and how much he had slowed down mentally and physically. He was so pleased to see us and wanted to relinquish everything that he had been doing. I could see that he was tired and not looking after himself as he used to do. When he insisted on driving me into town, as he would not let me use his car, I could see the fatigue in his eyes. I began to talk to him often about leaving his cottage and settling down with his new family in Devon. Although he was still upright and active, I was extremely worried about his future.

After I returned to India he did make that decision, distributing his possessions and moving down to Devon to live with my aunt. Once he blacked out on a friends' lawn after driving a long distance and he gave up driving immediately. After years of receiving long airmail letters with his graceful sloping writing, I was shocked to receive letters that had become faint and illegible and he finally wrote to say that he was not going to write again. He was eighty years old. In the next few years, I travelled to see him whenever I could, taking Alpana with me. He suffered a stroke that affected his speech and on each visit I could see the change. He was growing tired and found it difficult to converse, often looking at me with dreadful vacant eyes. In small flashes he was his old self, still the person I had looked up to all my life. I summoned the courage to ask him if he minded that I was so far away, a mute appeal for forgiveness I suppose, but he answered quite calmly and like his old self, that he considered himself lucky to have seen us for the past four summers. 'I have so many memories,' he said, and 'and no one can take them away.' As willingly as he relinquished me for my marriage so he relinquished me again, and I have no words to express the magnanimity of his gesture.

And then that day in Shillong when Dee rang . . . The flight to London and the bus journey to Exeter all passed as in a dream. It was two days to Christmas. My cousin Vicki held my hand when she took me to the funeral parlour where my father lay. But it was not my father that I saw, so quiet and still. Someone had too carefully trimmed his bushy eyebrows and clipped his moustache when he could no longer protest. The familiar hands were worst of all, too scrubbed, mute and unnatural, lying on the white satin coverlet inside the coffin, which was not his style at all. The room was very cold and there was an artificial perfume in the air. I knew he was not there at all. A strange vicar presided over the funeral service at the crematorium, calling my father by his first name, one he rarely used. Perhaps it would not have worried him as it worried me. I did not want his name and the fact that he lived and died to pass so quickly into oblivion, to be conveniently wiped out. I wanted somewhere on a simple stone, the dates of his birth and death to be engraved with the words that he had been a beloved father, so that our children, or strangers reading them, would see in a few lines the evidence of his life.

I was surprised at how many strangers in the small town stopped me to say that they were sorry to hear of my father's death, and that they wished they had been allowed to pay their respects at his funeral. They were his neighbours or the shopkeepers whom he used to meet on his short walks to buy newspapers or the sweets that had replaced his pipe. One of them said that she used to watch him going for walks with his stick to inspect a hole being dug in the road by a young suntanned lad. She was anxious, she said, as she did not know how the youngster would respond. But they always discussed its progress with mutual respect, and she would sigh with relief as he went slowly on his way. My father would never have been patronizing as he would have assessed the effort taken to make it and the young man responded to some unspoken experience that they seemed to share, as they wished each other a civilized good day. It is an image of my father that I treasure.

If he had lived until the following March he would have been eighty-nine. Our birthdays were only a day apart. In all the years of knowing him I had only dared to oppose him twice. Once I had not been able to accept his statement that pottery should be mass produced to suit a common taste and once I had defended my younger brother fiercely. In the latter case, when I returned to my room in Liverpool I found a bowl of azaleas delivered through Interflora, with a small note in his own handwriting saying that I was right and he had been in the wrong. He was always supportive of what I wished to do. For me, his fresh uncomplicated link with an outdoor life represented all that was safe and honourable.

A most private and complex man, he may have seemed to others to have beaten a personal retreat and narrowed his horizons down to his immediate family, but I always believed that he saw the world around him with enough of a direct gaze, even if he excluded the possibility of tragedy from his mind. In his relationships with others, those closest to him, he was sometimes at his worst, and yet many who loved him recognized that he was upright not only in his stance, but also in his nature. In his personal affairs, all that his father envisaged for him fell away. It was a surprise to be shown a photograph of him as a young man on the ski slopes of Davos and to be told that others envied his fortune and his life style. I realized there was a part of him that I had never known at all.

When the time came to pack his personal belongings, I did so myself, as I could not bear the exposure of his private life to indifferent eyes. When I finally had to open his top bureau drawers I did so with a pang of guilt. Amongst his ties and hankies lay a lifetime of all that had meant much for him. Crudely embroidered gifts from my schooldays . . . a note from me thanking them for a Christmas, underneath which my father had written in pencil that it was from a daughter so remote that they hardly knew her at all.

However inarticulate we may have been towards each other, I know that for most of my life, he formed its base and he occupied so much of my subconscious thought that everything I did was somehow related to him, as a compass needle is drawn to the North. And when I think of him, as I often do, I remember that he kept all darkness at bay by his love of simple pleasures, painting a door, cementing a wall or digging his garden. I think of his deep delight in waking up to a fine morning and for myself, at least, no unnecessary expectations, but that I share the morning with him.

DIGGING

Today I think
Only with scents—scents dead leaves yield,
And bracken , and wild carrot's seed,
And the square mustard field;

Odours that rise
When the spade wounds the root of tree
Rose, currant, raspberry or goutweed,
Rhubarb or celery;

The smoke's smell, too,
Flowing from where a bonfire burns
The dead, the waste, the dangerous,
And all to sweetness turns.

It is enough
To smell, to crumble the dark earth,
While the robin sings over again
Sad songs of Autumn mirth.
                    —Edward Thomas, killed in action 1917.

■

HUBERT ALAN SPENCE THOMAS

BORN 7 MARCH 1899
DIED 21 DECEMBER 1987

Chapter Five

Unfinished Business
Sonal Shukla

During the course of the several drafts that I had to make in writing about my father, I was asked to give a talk on him. A composer and a poet, my father was something of a celebrity in the world of Gujarati arts and culture during the fifties and the sixties. He had now turned seventy-five and a newly formed cultural association decided to honour him at a special function. I was to speak, of course, from personal experience as his daughter, while some well-known musicians, poets and other prominent persons were to speak about his work. 'I'll have to mention only the good parts,' I told my father. He laughed. I repeated these words in my speech and the audience laughed too. However, I knew that I was actually trying to assure myself, my father and the audience, in the garb of cheeky humour, that I was only being diplomatic and not dishonest. I don't think the audience cared one way or the other or my father really caught what I meant, but I was uneasy that I was going on record saying nice things while, in reality, I was seething in anger recalling all the unfinished business of youth with him.

As I was preparing that speech I vividly recalled how cruel, negligent and self-centred he had been, seeking only his pleasure with his second wife, and being totally indifferent to the plight of his daughters—all three coping with the trials of adolescence and traumatized by the sudden loss of their mother. It was frustrating that by the time I had distanced myself and had become strong enough emotionally to deal with him, he had grown old and feeble, charming, playful and childlike once again. Memories that had endeared him to us came back to me as I settled down to write.

I saw him as a product of his own socioeconomic environment and realized how much he had transcended its narrow, chauvinistic beliefs and attitudes and how much all of us, especially we sisters, had benefited from it. His own childhood had been none too good. He lost his mother when he was six. His father ventured into the film industry as a producer and director, kept a series of mistresses, earned and blew up large sums of money, incurred debts; became an alcoholic and then a drug addict, before suffering a severe paralytic stroke while still in his forties. It must have been a lonely childhood, especially after his grandmother died when he was twelve. But he was never bitter about his father. Occasionally he would relate some incidents of anxiety and deprivation with a little sadness but he usually talked of his father with indulgence and fondness. Apparently, the old man had a lot of charm and a great sense of humour as my father recalled; by all accounts, he was very adventurous. But he could not have been much of a father. That may be why my father has a bit of 'a little boy lost' in him—one of his best poems is about a boy who is let down by his father. It is quite unlike his better known songs.

I remembered all those songs that he wrote for us, relieved that here, at last, was some material that I could comfortably talk about and the audience would love. After all they were gathering to hear about and applaud a creative person. Yes, my father wrote songs and skits specially for us. He read out poems and prose pieces of great authors to us, and he created lovely, exciting children's stories as he narrated them to us. He invented games, taught us to speak in rhyme, in alliteration, in new kinds of phrases and bought—together with our mother—lots and lots of books. These are treasures that nobody can take away from us. How did he get all those books? Where did he look for them? We owned a thousand books in the early fifties when there was not much by way of children's literature in Gujarati except Dakshinamurti publications and translations of Jules Verne's books.

We loved our father. And we hated and feared our mother in various degrees. Papa—as we called him—was our pal, our playmate, whereas she was Authority. Harsh, punishing, cold and unfair, though also perceptive and brilliant. She was always reading something even though she was frequently in bed with some illness. What we did not know at the time was that she was steadily going mad, not the least because her marriage had not worked out and was finally breaking up. I remember her withdrawing more and more into herself, except when she picked up a quarrel with my father at night; about being broke all the time, about his not having heeded her warnings against a partner who finally cheated him, and later about his growing affair with an aspiring young singer. The singer was to be his second wife after my mother's sudden death at the age of thirty-seven. It was a classic case of a heart attack following a broken heart.

My mother had burnt her bridges behind her in the very first year of college when she gave up a promising academic career to elope with my father. Young people, especially women, did not choose whom to marry in the India of the thirties. Although both came broadly under the category of Brahmins, the difference in the subcastes was so great that traditionally they would not have been allowed to marry or even to share food with each other. My father belonged to the upper Brahmin caste of Nagars in Gujarat, a highly literate community of microscopic size. They had contributed substantially to modern Gujarati literature well before Independence. They were the first to acquire a knowledge of Persian and had served as administrators under the Rajputs, Muslims and Marathas; later came the acquisition of English and the entry into modern professions.

Father came from an impoverished landlord family in the state of Baroda. His father had been a college dropout, and he himself had been unable to go to college because my wayward grandfather had failed to pay his fees. It appears that my father played the flute, chewed tobacco and pursued my mother with steadfastness against her brothers' wishes.

My mother came from a semirural place in Saurashtra and belonged to what I assume was a basically conservative family, although her mother was a school principal and later a school inspector—highly unusual in those days. We had very little to do with my mother's family as they had practically disowned her. Only two of her brothers kept in touch with her while she lived and, after her death, with us sisters. One of them had brought her to Bombay because English education was not available in her native place. My father fondly remembers how she used to mispronounce English words when she first came to Bombay and how fast she picked up English and higher level maths.

It was this same uncle of mine who had brought my father and his younger brother to Bombay after their grandmother's death. This uncle was a friend of my grandfather. He was a good deal older than both my parents, and my father addressed him as uncle too. We had a great time when he visited us because he would indulge us, our parents being too respectful to protest. Fond as my maternal uncle had been of my father, he thought him quite unsuitable as a husband for his sister because he was not highly educated and did not have a steady job. I remember from snatches of conversations in the family that my father had worked as a farmer, and had even raised poultry to earn a livelihood after his marriage. This was in U.P. where a relative owned a lot of land. My parents made it sound like great fun. After the owner sold the farm, they came back to Bombay where my father first became a playback singer and then a music director with moderate success in the forties.

I grew up in a medium-size apartment in a middle-class suburb. Apart from a piano that must have been there for professional reasons, we had leather sofa sets, a radiogram and curtains on the windows—the kind of things that our neighbours did not have. I suppose we were slightly better off and more westernized than the rest. Nor did we observe any food taboos or religious rites and rituals.

For a long time I was supposed to be my father's girl, his special child and, perhaps, a son that he did not have. This surprises me today because I feel no special bond with him. I am fond of him in a mild sort of a way but feel no need to seek his approval for my efforts, the way my younger sister does. Nor do I have the intense commitment to him that my elder sister has. I was—and still am, they tell me, although I am long past the age when she died—the spitting image of my mother. And like her I am articulate and assertive. My mother couldn't stand me.

My father's family made much of the fact that I was not light-skinned like my sisters or my mother. It is in this context that my father seems to have declared me his favourite. I used to feel this was an act of kindness and was duly grateful to him. And really he was often kind-hearted, only you could not tell how long that mood would last. He could become quite self-absorbed as we all noticed. I knew from a fairly young age that my mother had wanted an abortion when she conceived me but my father had insisted on having another child. I was grateful to him for this too—well, I owed him my very existence, didn't I? Today, as a feminist, I empathize with my mother. Why would she have wanted another baby in barely two years? At that time they were absolutely broke. My father named me Sonal, meaning golden, then a very unusual name. Later it became very popular among gold-loving Gujaratis. So I owed my father my very being, my name and my status in the family.

For a long time I could not resolve my conflicting feelings about my father. Even now I sometimes wish he was not so self-absorbed and indifferent. Then I see other women—for instance—some of my former schoolmates, who have had very attentive parents, conscientious but authoritative fathers who made decisions for them and loving but orthodox mothers who trained them to fit into the established mould. I am thankful that Papa always let us be. He could not, and after his second marriage would not, provide more than the bare minimum for us but we were free to choose what we wanted to study, take up any job that came our way and marry whom we chose. Bless him, I don't think it ever even occurred to him that women should not have decision-making powers. Both my parents were liberals to beat all liberals, except that my father was not likely to have known about liberalism as a political philosophy.

A trait that I have admired in my father is his commitment to work, though not in terms of sticking to some boring monotonous routine. It is the enthusiasm he feels and the enormous hard work he can put in. By the time I was ten or so, his financial situation had become pretty grim. When I was eleven, my name was struck off the school register because he could not pay the monthly fee of six rupees. My elder sister had already been taken off the school register a couple of years earlier. Our family was in social disgrace because even the grocer and the milkman had not been paid for months. But unlike my mother he did not brood or become unproductive. He composed music even when nobody wanted it, he wrote poetry, translated hundreds of poems of medieval saint-poets from colloquial Hindi, studied Sanskrit and religious texts. Even after his retirement from his job as a music producer with All India Radio, he took pleasure in his arduous efforts to study Sanskrit. Most people did not understand that his interest in religious texts, poetry and philosophy was merely cultural. He was never a religious person in the sense practising Hindus are. I have never known him to refer to God in personal terms, except as a figure of speech, even though he has written some beautiful *bhajans* and drawn from religious epics from time to time to write musicals. He did have an on and off relationship for many years with a gurulike person whom he merely called Motabhai or Elder Brother. Finally they parted ways because my father found the man to be too narrow in his outlook. In a rare criticism of this man he said that he could not take the unreasonableness of it all. Motabhai was a supporter of Hindu communalism which my father could not accept. Why it took him so many years to realize this is beyond me. To me the man had always appeared a bore with his vague ideas and pointless talk. He was bossy and autocratic but treated my father affectionately. My elder sister felt he was a father substitute. I don't know. My mother had not liked him and my stepmother resented him too. Was he, like the daughters, some kind of a balancing factor in his marriage? For I feel quite convinced that we were that in his worst years with my mother. How else can I explain his complete metamorphosis after our mother's death?

The change in him was sudden and abrupt. Now he seemed preoccupied when he came home. He was critical of a lot of things we did. I came in for reproof, for not managing the house well. We were not allowed to mourn our mother, and though we loved him better and had been scared of our mother's hysterics, we missed her too. Often we missed his warmth and attention more than we missed our mother. I think he was in a turmoil. He wanted to remarry as soon as he could. A few days after my mother's death he told my elder sister that he was planning to remarry. Since she was aware of his involvement with the other woman, she was pained but not surprised. I had never believed in my mother's accusations and hated her for talking in this manner about our father. My sister kept this knowledge to herself for a few weeks. Then she told me that this woman had gone to her native place to seek her mother's permission to marry my father and that my father was receiving letters from her. They were kept in an attache case that was locked. We opened it and read the letters. I was shocked to learn that I had been wrong all along and my mother had been right. But the letters also provided us with a lot of amusement. I was about to reach my teens. We giggled at our father being referred to as a rose (sketched as a rose in one of the letters) and other romantic endearments.

From then on, like Papa, we would also wait for the postman to arrive. We raided an old trunk that my sister said contained letters of other couples in our family and we found a treasure trove. There were letters between our parents, grandparents and great grandparents on the paternal side and paternal great grandmother's mother and her husband—old letters tied in a cloth and preserved. I still remember the highly dramatic endearments like

Queen of My Heart (*hridayeshwari*) and King of My Soul (*prannath*) though very little else. We must have messed up the attache case for my father grew suspicious. He asked me if I had opened it. I said, 'No.' He reminded me that I never lied to him. I said, 'Yes, I did not.' That was the first lie I ever told him and I am sure he must have known it. Next year when he went to Benaras he took the packet of old letters with him and submerged them in the Ganga, saying it was wrong to read about parents' romances and he did not wish anybody including himself to be tempted to read those letters. It is a great pity because, though we were not aware at the time, it was a rare collection containing letters written by nineteenth-century women in Gujarat.

Four months after my mother's death, Father remarried. A year and a half before that he had begun to recover from financial disaster. He had a couple of assignments for film music and then a position as a music producer on All India Radio. I was sent back to school, but my elder sister could not go back because she had lost too many years. She completed her education as an external student later. While my father was on his honeymoon I managed to enrol my younger sister and myself in two totally new schools that were coming up. I changed schools because I was too ashamed to go back to my class where my friends would ask me about my father's remarriage. They had all come to share my grief and treated me with consideration after my mother's death. I think children and young adults have a special regard for someone who has seen death at close quarters or lost a parent. But I also knew they would gossip and some of them would ask me uncomfortable questions. It was best to go to new surroundings I decided. I had that kind of initiative. I had also learnt to turn away creditors when they came to demand payment, get groceries on credit, and so on, and even, on some occasions, to borrow small sums for my parents during our period of financial distress, and I had kept daily accounts before Father's remarriage.

A period of emotional isolation and deprivation began from this point. So far either the whole family enjoyed financial security and the benefits of a regular income or everybody starved. Now according to the new rules, the monthly family expenses and repayments of old debts were to come from my fathers's salary and our stepmother's income was for her own expenses and savings. This created two different standards of living in the family. As our expenses were to come out of our father's earnings, we were told there was barely anything for clothes and pocket money, though our father as breadwinner and the head of the family was to be allowed certain privileges: he would get a first class railway pass for local travel whereas we, when we went to college, would travel by third class even though we could get 50 percent concession rates as students. Or he would get to eat vegetables while we ate watery dal. Our childhood pal was now the head of the family. We felt orphaned. Perhaps to cope with guilt feelings he began to make us feel silly and inadequate. When we sisters fought with each other or argued with him he would say that the days of domestic strife were over in his household, obliquely referring to our mother's 'nagging'. No open reference was ever made to her. But we three sisters obviously recalled her existence.

To be fair, my stepmother has her points. She is always very good with little children and the sick. She has a beautiful voice and sound business sense. But she was competing against a ghost. She felt the need to justify her affair with my father and talked of my mother having been a shrew, that she had not maintained her figure and physical charms, and so on. Our mother had been moody and often violently abusive to us in her last years, whereas our stepmother fits very well with the established standards of feminine behaviour. But her convictions about what are due to our mother's daughters are very strong, and our father has always gone along with them, and there have been times when we minded our father's acquiescence. She made it clear that we would not be given any jewellery or even a wedding sari as a present when we got married because our mother's jewellery was sold off during lean times. When my younger sister's son was born rather late in her life; this only grandchild of my parents was not given even the customary token piece of silver or gold. Apart from heartburn, these actions caused us loss of face among friends and in-laws. Even the poorest of our friends received something from their parents as a token of affection.

The worst memory I have is the method she devised to wake me up when my father and she returned late from a party or a rehearsal. My elder sister was away in Benaras to appear externally for the school-leaving exams as it was my stepmother herself who had wisely encouraged my father to send her there to stay with his brother. My younger sister and I slept like logs at night. Once when they returned from a late show, they kept knocking but neither of us woke up, whilst their knocking aroused the whole neighbourhood! We did not have an electric bell or a latchkey then. We used a padlock and whoever left last would leave the key with the next door neighbour during the daytime as this was the normal custom in the suburbs. Our apartment was on the ground floor and had two entrances. We could have locked the main door, entered from the other door, closed it and slept peacefully, if they had made a duplicate key. But no. To save on that expense, an original idea was put into action. I was to tie a rope around my leg and fasten the other end to a window bar; when they returned they would pull the rope so that I would wake up and open the door. I would be groggy with sleep and so would walk with the rope still around my leg, stumble, fall, sit up, untie the rope and then open the door. It was most annoying and humiliating but I could do nothing about it as I had neither the money nor the power to get a new lock or a duplicate key. I don't think my stepmother deliberately meant to humiliate me. In her mind, this must have been quite normal and she recently related these as humorous episodes, laughing as she described how the rope was fastened around my leg. She could not understand why I was upset by this memory. But how could my father not understand? I would argue with him, try to prove my point, demand justice, cry, sob, sulk only to be branded aggressive and hysterical by both of them. I think he was trying to buy peace and harmony, at any cost, it was his last chance. If his daughters' emotional and material needs came in the way, he treated them as obstacles.

He became a closed person, inaccessible to us, coming out of his shell briefly when we were ill or when the mood suited him. We would bend backwards to please him, to get him to say something, to make some gesture that would make us feel authentic and legitimize our existence, usually to no avail. These conflicting feelings about him, letting me down when I most needed his support, compared to the earlier memories of a loving and sensitive father, bothered me for many years even after I married, until I understood sexual politics within the family. When things were very bad between our mother and him, he needed his daughters as his allies, our mutual love and affection must have been a welcome relief in stressful times. Our mother knew him only too well and had seen through him; I presume he did not like her intellectual abilities, although I remember the times when they were happy with each other before the start of their final conflict over his involvement with another woman. Mine was not the only family where children, pets and servants liked the master of the house best. We really loved him. However, he no longer needed us as allies after our mother died. I feel that he did not do any of this consciously, he was merely seeking his peace and happiness. Later, in his old age he admitted to me that he had allowed certain things to pass as otherwise my stepmother would nag him. I was struck by the expression! Hadn't they used the same term for our mother, maintaining that her misery was her own creation? But I must admit he has a reasonably good marriage and a creative relationship with his second wife.

My father continued to remain remote and withdrawn, occasionally emerging out of his shell. He was very sweet and helpful when I was hospitalized after a bus accident, visiting me daily with home-cooked food. All the same he and my stepmother took away a large part of the paltry sum I received as compensation for a permanent scar and disability on my hand, a fact that enraged my husband. My father went through a lot of trouble to visit my elder sister regularly in Ahmedabad after an accident in the kitchen left her with severe burns. He was very supportive of her and encouraged her to get a divorce because her in-laws were oppressive and her husband weak. He brought her back to Bombay. After that he left it entirely to her to somehow earn a living and pay for her studies, her clothes and other needs, and also contribute towards household expenses. But when my younger sister's marriage broke up, he could not take it. For my elder sister, he might have felt responsible since he had arranged her marriage, the only arranged marriage in our entire family. But my younger sister had made her own choice. Her husband and his family were not bad in any way. He was angry when my sister had problems of incompatibility. He refused to see her for the next three years, then in an about turn he welcomed her back. This was typical of him. He would make a good gesture but you could not rely upon it because he would then withdraw all support, at times he would give a small sum for a school picnic but the next time he would refuse, saying the hot sun was bad for one's health. Sometimes he would laugh with us and at other times he would turn cold and nasty. Once when he heard about my younger sister's trouble he told me to ask her if she needed financial help. I felt gratified and he must have noticed it for he hastily added, 'Only a small sum, please. I do not have unlimited resources.' I kept quiet. In our worst crisis we had never asked him for so much as a rupee. I was not going to mention his offer to my sister. I think his nerve was broken after his near bankruptcy in the early years, and his second wife constantly reminded him and others how he had no money and only debts when she married him. For the first time in his life he was developing notions of security and possessiveness. He and my mother were always very generous in a bohemian style; you can't live in that way and survive, he must have concluded. I had coined a term for his ups and downs in good moods, not just about money but about his receptivity and warmth, 'standing on a *machan*' (raised platform). There is a folktale prefacing the famous *Thirty-two Tales of the Royal Throne* which begins this way.

> King Bhoj was passing through some fields with his entourage. He was incognito. A farmer was standing on a *machan* in his field. He saw the group of travellers and called out to invite them to have a glass of fresh sugarcane juice. As the entourage arrived, the farmer got down from the scaffold to cut sugarcane but he could not bring himself to cut any as he felt that he would be giving away his hard-earned product. With folded hands he expressed regrets that the sugarcane in his field was not ripe enough to squeeze. He mounted the *machan*. Yet again as the travellers were going away he called them and pleaded that they should not leave without enjoying his hospitality. After the party returned, the same routine was repeated and he apologized for having to send them away. Then once again he climbed up on the *machan* and the same scenario was repeated. Bhoj felt there was something underneath the *machan* that changed the farmer when he climbed atop. The king ordered the people too dig underneath, and lo, a beautiful golden throne was found. It was studded with the most expensive jewels. There were sixteen steps leading to the actual throne, with two female statues on either side of each step. As Bhoj began to mount the throne, the first statue spoke out, 'Are you as brave and generous as King Vikramaditya whose throne you are trying to climb onto?' Bhoj asked what she meant and she narrated a story of Vikramaditya's good deeds.

Thirty-two stories of a good king are woven together in this way. And I sometimes felt I must dig the ground underneath when Papa was being good.

The last time I had a confrontation with him was when my brother was getting married. My brother is his only child from the second marriage, and I knew my stepmother would want to buy the customary jewellery for the bride. Having spent ten years in a joint family after marriage I had learnt how elders try to cover up some crucial lapses without admitting to any favouritism on their part. We are all very attached to our brother, the baby of the family. We sisters did not want anything any longer, but I was interested to see how the principle of not giving anything to the bride would be observed now. It wasn't. A week before the wedding, my father presented three of us with a cheque of five thousand rupees each. My younger sister and I refused our cheques and asked why he was giving us the money. He had no answer. I said they were free to give whatever they liked to my brother and his wife but they should not try to make up for having hurt us when we were young. He insisted that the amount was not related to the wedding, became a bit melodramatic and practically prostrated himself, pleading with us to accept the cheques. There was not much point in arguing with him so we took them. At the age of forty it did not make sense to me to take anything from my father.

Am I being too harsh and judgemental? Is he a God that failed? Doesn't every father set himself up as God? What about my own failings? When he watched television constantly during his seventies, I was upset because he and my mother had tried to keep us away from cheap entertainment. (How we had longed to see the popular Hindi films that our friends saw! As adults we would talk snobbishly of the Tagore plays we had seen and the classical music concerts we had attended!) As I grow older, I catch myself watching TV on some pretext or the other. On his part, in his eighties, my father has discovered Amy Tan, Alice Walker and Sara Parteskey and, what is more, despite his failing eyesight plans to catch up on feminist poetry!

And so, it is all over. Nothing spectacular has happened, but I realize I have already reached middle age and after all he is only an old man, living his own life quietly and unobtrusively. There is no conflict, nothing left to settle.

Chapter Six

Let Colours Speak
Rekha Rao

From an early age, I had this inexplicable need to draw and paint. It had a lot to do with my father being an artist. We lived in a house filled with canvasses and colours; our home crackled with culture and creative energy. Painters, writers, dancers, musicians dropped by, stayed on an hour, a day or seven days. It was and still is an open house.

As a young boy Papa used to paint and draw from memory. He used any available means like lamp soot, red pebbles ground in gum water to paint on the walls of their hut in the village of Kattingeri in south Karnataka. After his father's death, his mother determined to get the best art education for her son, moved to Bombay, where his elder brother, Anantram, was already settled. Papa joined a private art institute while working part-time at Koparde's Photo Studio. He later joined and graduated from the J.J. School of Art and taught for a year. His sojourn in France at the Ecole des Beaux Arts and in other European countries had a significant impact on his thoughts and in turn influenced his style of painting. This was a stepping stone for an enriching and memorable long innings in the field of contemporary art in India.

In the early years, Papa was a struggling artist and life was hard, with no proper workplace nor a steady income to maintain a wife and three children. Papa's workplace was part of our home, art materials were my playthings. None of us felt the lack of any comforts. One day the landlady refused to renew the lease of our flat; there was great tension in the air and that same evening Papa's close friend, Velkar, offered us his bungalow at Mahableshwar, a hill station in Maharashtra. Papa accepted it and the family moved along with him.

Mahableshwar has specially rich memories for me. Every day, we would walk around the hills, he with his sketch pad and I with just the wonder of a child. Back home while he returned to his easel and canvases, my field of action was paper and a dozen poster colours. Impressions of villagers, the weekly market, fields of strawberries, cows and goats formed the subject matter. Every day I used to paint and run over to show him my work. He was always full of praise and never touched or corrected my work. Now and then he would go through the lot when I was not around, keep the good paintings and discard the rest. I watched this slyly from behind the curtains but never uttered a word. The day would not come to an end till he had told us a story, an imaginative one filled with owls, bats and foxes.

On festival days, Papa and I would go to the village community hall in the evenings and he would paint the faces of the villagers and transform them into Rama, Laxman and Hanuman with his colour-soaked brushes. The villagers then took out floats on bullock carts in a procession down the main street. On those occasions, I felt the actors were filled with a spirit of pure divinity—fighting Ravana and the forces of evil. The colours conferred on the different characters the attributes each one in his secret heart desired most. That was a fruitful year for both Papa and me, as we painted for hours on end. I remember walking with Papa in Mahableshwar, when we came across a blind man being led by an old woman holding a stick. Later that day, I painted the scene and Papa noticed that the man had no eyes. He questioned me about that and was startled when his five-year old replied that he had explained that the man could not see, so what was the use of drawing eyes on his face? Recalling our Mahableshwar days, Papa said to a friend: ' I was always able to draw inspiration from my children. They have taught me so much, what with their novel perceptions of the world. My daughter Rekha was such a child whose view ceaselessly refreshed my own artistic perspective. I remember, when en route to Mahableshwar, she spotted a bamboo tree and remarked how akin its "tall and thin" shape was to her father's. Wasn't I too as tall and slender as it was? It was the first time that her sense of imagination and artistic approach validated itself to me.'

A rope tied to an anjeer or fig tree served as a swing for me and my two siblings. Papa and Amma did not believe in sending us to any formal school at an early age. A year later we moved back to Mahim, a Bombay suburb, where my father finally got a studio and the family a tiny flat. In front of our house stood a huge pipal tree inhabited by thousands of cranes. Below was a tile factory bustling with activity, day and night. The workers celebrated Holi each year with songs and dances and plenty of *bhang*. We were invited to these celebrations and Papa and I were ever ready to join in their festivities.

To the left of the factory stood the Mahim Dargah, incredibly beautiful on moonlit nights. During the month of Ramazan, a very old man, bent with age, with wild dishevelled hair and shaking beard, used to go from house to house, knocking at the doors with his stick, waking the faithful before the crack of dawn. This and similar other images created strong impressions on our minds and we have painted similar subjects, in our own styles, through the years.

Around this time the entire family went along with Papa to Telwal near Mysore. UNESCO had organized an adult education drive by conducting field experiments to evolve the most suitable instructional material. Dr. Shivram Karanth was assigned the task of writing the book which he called *Jogi Kannda Uru* (The Village through the Eyes of a Mendicant). Papa illustrated this book in simple line drawings in his inimitable style. Several delegates from European and African countries participated in the camp. We were the only children there, but enjoyed every minute as we walked along with adults from village to village, watching them teach the simple villagers the joy of the written word and basic hygiene. One particular story I still remember, which my Papa and Amma frequently told the villagers was of Gautam Buddha, who was approached by an inconsolable mother with a dead baby in her arms, beseeching him to revive her child. And Buddha's calm advice was to go and get some mustard seeds from a house which death had not visited. The mother found solace in the realization that sorrow was universal. It had such an impact on our young minds that later on in our lives, we have been able to accept the loss of our grandparents and some of our friends with equanimity.

With the passage of time, intellectual process joined the emotional reactions to forms and colours and situations around me. Facing a blank canvas, Papa and I would discuss the problem and the ways of handling it. This then is the only form of art education I have had. Through the years, I have learnt to understand the tactile qualities of paint. Colour has the power to embody and invoke light within each painting. He often told me that a painting is not a literary exercise where the viewer has to be supplied with a long explanation. It is the story of the artist who has eyes and hands and feet as the rest, but whose vocabulary comprises the shapes, surface, texture and colour he puts on canvas.

Once, I recollect, returning from the gallery after seeing a particularly good exhibition of portraits, I felt a bit dejected for I had not learnt to paint in the Western academic style. Seeing my long drawn face, Papa at once dispelled my fears by insisting that I start drawing portraits from life, using my sister or girls next door as models. I did this for several weeks, even months. Papa explained to me why he had not insisted that I master this technique to begin with. He told me the story of Princess Usha, daughter of King Anirudha, in ancient India. One day the princess dreamt of a handsome prince, riding a white steed across the clouds. She fell in love with him and was determined to meet him. She summoned her maid Chitralekha and described the prince in her dream. Chitralekha drew a portrait of him, full of sensitivity, exuding the true character and bearing of a prince. This then was portrait painting in those days, where the prime consideration was *bhava*. Even today, those principles hold good, for a portrait that does not reflect the personality of the sitter is no portrait at all.

Papa is a strict disciplinarian. He lives an ascetic life. His wants are few and he has instilled in us a pride in whatever we do, a detachment too, which has helped us to take things as they come. Though ours is a Brahmin household, it is not an orthodox one. Papa does not believe in rituals, pujas and horoscopes. The only time a priest did come to our house was to perform my marriage ceremony, which was held in our backyard. Overnight, our artist friends transformed it into a beautiful pandal with *kolam* and flowers. The ceremony was short and just a few friends and relatives were present.

At times I feel that in spite of his progressive ideas, he lives in the past. He still thinks a hundred rupees is enough to run the house for a week. He is generous to a fault when it comes to dealing with his servants and helpers, but when my mother asks for some money he needs to know why. He lends money to all and sundry, knowing too well there is no chance of recovering it. Ours is the only household I know where no one can correct the servant. According to my father only his good points should be noted. Papa often chides us and my mother in front of the servants, which I have never been able to accept, especially when he does so to cover up the servants' faults. I often confront him on this issue, and his reply that he knows what poverty can do does not justify sloth and insolent behaviour from the subordinates.

His ideas regarding a woman's role in today's society at times seem outdated, at times too modern. On the one hand he is strict with my mother, and dictates almost everything, whilst with his daughters he is more reasonable and willing to listen. This is not because he is an indulgent father but because at times he is caught between two worlds: one in which he grew up, the other more liberal. Yet he does have an open mind, and it is easy to make him see another point of view.

Sometimes he expects me to be like him but I am differently made. After I got married he converted a room in his house into a studio for me. Now and then he would call me to see the progress of his work. At the end of it, my painting looked exactly like his! On days I did not paint he would go on and on about how I had wasted my day. I soon realized, I would have to look out for a studio elsewhere and I did.

Papa has taught me to see an image within every stone and rock. He reminds me often that art is meant to elevate people and not to drag them through the mire. For me, all the forces of life are dissolved in the varieties of colour. His words will always keep ringing in my ears, 'Let colours speak to you as inexplicably as music.'

■

After a creative and fruitful life, my father passed away peacefully on 26 March 1996, at the age of 84. Till the end he had a razor-sharp mind but a frail body. He left a rich legacy of art for posterity.

CHAPTER SEVEN

WHO WILL CHERISH US NOW?
Neela D'Souza

Writing about my father was not easy. On the third anniversary of his death I went through my routine chores with a running commentary of memory in my mind. Disjointed, unconnected, yet, as the years pass memories crystallize and define my own thought and feelings and attitudes.

He was authoritarian and patriarchal, as were most men of his generation. But he gave his children open minds and freedom to follow their inclinations. What better could I have asked for? Carl Marzani's words about his father in *The Education of a Reluctant Radical*[1] are what I would say myself: 'I love him deeply, though not blindly. Diligently, as I write about him, I have searched for his flaws and they were remarkably few.'

> Lovechild! The phrase would have sounded odd, archaic, had someone else used it. We would have nudged each other and smirked at the prim- and- properness of the idea. Who ever spoke of a lovechild these days? A child of love, born in love, born to be loved, generous in giving and sharing love: that was a lovechild. That was what the term seemed to imply. But a child born out of wedlock was a b—bandied and bruised and turned into an epithet, a term of abuse, a loose phrase that young men affected in their speech at a certain stage in their growing up. No overtones, not even a suggestion of love left.
> From Appa the term sounded right. Not right in the sense of being proper but natural, befitting. My very correct Appa with his love of propriety, his carefully chosen words— a lovechild!
> It was strange to see Appa with his head shaven. It gave him a quality I couldn't quite place or describe—humility, per-

haps? Not that Appa was an arrogant person. But he was so confident and sure of himself, quick in judgement, unerring in decision. He exuded determination and strength of character. There was purposefulness in his very stride, his brisk quick walk. You wouldn't imagine he had had a heart attack a bare year ago. Or that he was past fifty. He was a man who hated to dawdle, who hated this in others; he insisted on speed in whatever we did. But humility? I had not noticed that in him before. Perhaps he had not had time for humility. He was in a reminiscent mood that evening as we sat out in the deepening twilight. The house was stifling hot; it was warm outside and we thirsted for a stirring in the air, fanning ourselves, sipping cool *nimbu panis* spiked with mint, grumbling all the while at Madras' long hot summer. Appa sat a little apart, the severe simplicity of his thin muslin shirt and dhoti accentuating the formal symbol of mourning—his close-shaven head. Hands tucked under his chin, his thoughts were far away, had travelled back in time as he thought, and spoke about his mother, his early home, his difficult childhood.

I wrote that about Appa some years ago—his mother had just died—remembering how he had dramatically revealed the skeleton in the family cupboard. It had to do with Grandmother, who was born of a tempestuous alliance between Appa's grandmother and a wealthy upper caste landowner from the village; his mild grandfather had not protested and had taken back his errant wife and raised the child as his own. Appa described his mother as a 'lovechild', a term I never really have heard used and seldom have seen in print.

I would like to describe my father, not as he was at any fixed point in time or remembrance, rather as I recall impressions and incidents over more than fifty years of conscious memory. Even in my earliest recollections I remember the jaunty air about him, a jauntiness that I associated with him till he was well into his seventies, before a combination of heart disease, diabetes and atherosclerosis succeeded finally in slowing him down. He was a short man, five feet five inches perhaps, and carried himself with an easy assurance. He favoured walking sticks, and he had four or five of them arranged in the whatnot that stood near the front door in the many homes we had in different parts of the country.

I never associated a stick with old age or feebleness and wondered why friends remarked or teased when my husband occasionally sported one.

'Self-made' is a term I dislike as there is a tinge of smugness to it, but it is the closest to describing him. Appa made himself. He gave his children all he could, provided us with opportunities to explore and grow, to make the most of ourselves. Appa's exemplar was Napoleon, whom he admired greatly and held up to us as an ideal. Napoleon never wasted a minute of time; while he shaved he read and planned battle strategy. 'Impossible' didn't figure in Napoleon's dictionary. He had said there was no word like 'cannot' in the English language. Later, much later, I wondered, did Napoleon really speak English?

Books and learning were Appa's great love. His companionship and guidance stimulated our minds and intellectual growth. For all his early impoverished background, the deprivations he had suffered, he was never short of marvellous enterprising ideas for us. He left me to make my decisions but was not above some behind-the-scenes steering. At twenty, trapped in an infatuation that would have swept me into a disastrous marriage, he was wise enough to remain on the sidelines. 'I wish you had chosen someone more intelligent,' was his only comment. Then he came up with the grand idea of a summer in Europe before going to the USA to study journalism and saved me from drifting into an unwise decision. The Italian prelude, a three-month stay in Perugia, would give me poise and that certain indefinable something that is associated with European culture, or so Appa firmly believed. And so, while most of my friends and contemporaries were getting ready for marriage or, in the rare instance, looking for a job, I was preparing for Europe and America.

On the morning of my departure in early 1954, butterflies fluttered madly inside me. Assailed by last minute nervousness and anxiety I blurted out my fears to him. ' I will land in Naples without knowing a word of Italian—what will I do? How will I manage?' 'You will be all right', he said, supremely confident of his daughter's ability to take on Italy, Italian and Italians, and fend for herself in a strange country. And I was more than all right, landed in Naples firmly on my feet and enjoyed my Roman holiday as you can only when you are a naive twenty, brimming with enthusiasm and curiosity and confidence.

Undoubtedly Appa instilled that in me. He expected and took for granted that I would come out on top. I accepted this confidence and through some process of osmosis made it my own. In later years it was puzzling to have my children accuse me of expecting too much from them. It had not occurred to me to question Appa's confidence in me. Why wasn't I able to do that for my children? Perhaps my parenting skills were far below his.

My father had a razor-sharp mind, honed over the years by a natural curiosity and an eagerness to learn that stayed with him through his life. He read prodigiously himself and deluged my brother and me with books. I remember how we looked forward to that monthly trip to the bookshop in New Market in Calcutta when Appa would buy a load of books for the Customs recreation library; my brother and I would read whatever we could of these in addition to those Appa bought specifically for us: *Tom Brown's School Days*, a set of R.L. Stevenson, the Walter Scott novels, Tagore's stories, Sister Nivedita's *Cradle Tales of Hinduism*, the legends of King Arthur, Sarojini Naidu's poems—a wonderful heady mixture. There were no restrictions on our reading. Appa trusted us to stay away from whatever we could not comprehend.

Following a natural interest in books and reading I wanted to study English literature at university. We argued and discussed this as he felt I would benefit from history as my major; it would be useful later for writing or whatever else I chose to do and there was a wealth of literature in history which would satisfy my desire for reading. I let myself be persuaded and did not regret the switch, as it opened the doors to a whole new world which would have remained unknown, unexplored, had I taken English literature.

On my first day as an undergraduate at Presidency College, Madras, I met the professor of history, who asked if I was related to the Sattanathan of Maharajah's College, Trivandrum, and was delighted to find that I was his daughter. Appa had been his senior in college with a reputation for scholarship that had filled his juniors with awe and admiration. 'Your father had read every book in the library,' said the professor. I was sure that was no exaggeration. Appa was overjoyed when I topped the university in history. 'This is history repeating itself,' he said with fond pride, as he had stood first in the university himself at the same examination and in the same subject in the twenties. We won the same prizes, and it thrilled him to think of two Sattanathans, a generation apart, listed somewhere in the records of the University of Madras. Someone, some day, would take note.

When Appa was growing up, a boy from his community, his village, finishing school and going to college was quite unheard of. He was looked upon as something of a marvel. Appa's village was Shencottah, near the foothills of the Western Ghats in Tirunelveli district, deep down in South India. Neither of his parents was literate. They were Padayachis of the Vanniyar backward class and very poor. Although not in as desperate a situation as the Dalits, the Vanniyars did suffer a good deal of social discrimination; they were mainly agricultural labourers, and in some cases cultivated their own land. My grandmother's family owned a small piece of land and being the only child she and her husband inherited it. The income from the land was utterly inadequate to feed the family so grandfather fell back on the family vocation as a musician. He played some sort of a wind instrument and formed a troupe with his brothers and other male relatives to perform at temple festivals, wedding processions and religious ceremonies. They were paid in rice, vegetables, dal, coconuts and oil. If it were a Brahmin or upper caste wedding, there would additionally be baskets of cooked food from the marriage feast; then everyone in the house ate well for a few days.

With his experience of poverty in all its manifestations and also of taboos of caste and caste professions, grandfather did not want his son to be a musician. He had aspirations to a petty government job for him; that would bring in a steady income and enable the family to free itself from poverty and discrimination, even move upwards socially. He was determined to educate his son. My father described his initiation into learning on Saraswati Puja at the end of *Navaratri*, when he was taught to say *'Om nama shivaya'*. The teacher selected by his family then held his hand and helped him trace the the first letter of the Tamil alphabet on sand. That would have been in 1910. I remember when my younger sister was five, we had a similar ceremony at home on Saraswati Puja when she sat on Appa's lap and he guided her little hand in forming the letter on a *thali* spread with *vibhuti*.

Appa went to the government elementary school which taught in Malayalam; this was the beginning of his bilingual fluency as the family was Tamil-speaking, but he spoke both the languages with ease. He was a quiet child, not very robust in health. Grandfather's silent stubborn resolve to educate his son laid down a strict regimen; play was excluded. Appa was allowed no fun with pebble and sticks, no *gilli-danda* or its Tamil equivalent, no flying kites—all that was a waste of time and would distract him from his studies. So eager was grandfather to see his son matriculate that he decided to hasten the learning process and Appa was somehow hustled into the English-medium school in Form 1 ahead of others of his age. This was a Christian missionary institution in a nearby village and it meant Appa living with relatives and later with his grandmother, who was sent to keep house and look after him. For a while he lived with an older sister who had been married when she was eleven. It was an unhappy marriage, she was treated as a slave in her husband's home. Appa witnessed the quarrels, which were all too frequent. He was deeply affected by her death when she was only twenty-two.

It was a hard life for a child; breakfast of fermented rice and whatever was left over from the previous night's meal, a two-mile trudge to and back from school with a little rice wrapped in a leaf to serve as lunch, no playmates or companions in the evenings. Father didn't talk much about his childhood or his young manhood except for an occasional testy remark like how he had weakened his eyes straining at his books by the dim light of a kerosene lamp, far into the night. Those details sounded theatrical, almost. Reading his autobiographical notes, after his death, brought all that painfully close. His childhood world had been so very different, so far removed from the comfort and care and happiness of ours, the world he gave us. My own acquaintance with village life in South India is minimal, and Appa's early years brought to mind scenes out of Dickens, almost another world, another age. The picaresque lightheartedness of R. K. Narayan's Swami growing up with his friends in Malgudi that drew instant delighted response from my children, belonged to their world and time.

I marvelled at that little boy from Shencottah, where did he get his fortitude, how did he develop the strength of character and purpose, the grit that saw him through those early years? There were moments of tranquillity. Appa describes sitting on a small platform in the family field just before harvest time, chasing away crows and flocks of little birds from the ripening grain; coming back from the daily bath in the stream holding his damp *dhoti* aloft on upraised arms like a sail; the colours of twilight, the evening breeze. He studied at home by the light of an oil lamp, trying to shut out the chatter of his younger siblings and intruding household noises, learnt Tamil, Malayalam and English and prepared for high school in the nearest town.

As he would have to be sent there as a boarder, the family needed to raise Rs.15 a month for his expenses. Where would it come from? The lovechild connection was resurrected and tapped. Grandmother took Appa to the family of the wealthy landowner, long dead now, which agreed to provide the funds. They financed his university education too. There were several brothers in the family who were interested in Appa because of his academic prowess; they showed some consideration and sympathy, though this was not unmixed with disdain. Repeated visits had to be made to their house to ask for and collect the money. Appa writes of hours of waiting in silent supplication, the feelings of frustration and humiliation as he stood outside on the verandah till someone of the family took notice of him. He writes of his thoughts on charity in the abstract, his mental agony and bitterness while waiting for charity to be doled out to him. But resolution was building within him even as he waited. Out of these experiences he developed a strong sense of filial duty and obligation to the family that placed so much hope and trust in him. He was determined to succeed.

For Appa, success was spelt out in material things. I remember arguments in my adolescent days, my accusation, 'You worship material success, money and position.' He countered, 'How else would you measure success? How else would I have been able to give you all a good education and the comforts you have?' Was it just fate that led my father through high school, college in Trivandrum where he performed brilliantly at university, and to a job in an all-India service so that we grew up away from the confines of Shencottah, even South India? Appa's career in the Customs and Central Excise and later in the Central Board of Revenue took us to many different parts of the country. Shencottah was a distant place in more ways than one, and the early annual visits to his village petered out by the time I was ten or eleven. It was a penance to spend the summer vacation there, feeling awkward and ill at ease. I was never happy in those unfamiliar surroundings, never close to my cousins and grandparents, and we didn't seem to have anything in common apart from family relationships. Perhaps our mother protested? Visits to Shencottah became infrequent and short. Appa went whenever he could, sometimes accompanied by Amma when they found someone to look after us.

We saw a great deal of the country through my father's regular transfers every three years or so. It meant changing schools, making new friends, adapting to new environments. But travelling was fun and Appa made it all seem easy and natural. His career advanced, spurred on by his natural ability and talent and desire for success. In 1947 when he was forty-two, Appa went as the Indian delegate to the Narcotic Drugs Commission of the United Nations and was elected president of the session at Lake Success in New York. Other distinctions followed. He had travelled a long way from Shencottah.

I remained unaware of his love for Tamil literature, a love that none of his children could really share with him as our education was of the missionary school type and made hybrids of us, talking and even thinking in English, though we always spoke Tamil at home. In the fifties when Appa was head of the Customs in Bombay he was invited to be president of the Tamil Sangham, the cultural association of Tamil-speaking people in the city. With his usual enthusiasm and drive he revved up the organization, and my mother and I were plunged into a spate of cultural evenings. I went along to see the drama festival he organized and had my first glimpse of contemporary Tamil theatre with its astonishing versatility. The beautifully decorated silver bowl that the Tamil Sangham presented to him when he left Bombay was a proud possession, which he gifted to me when he died.

During one of our annual visits to our grandparents in Shencottah, I learnt Tamil at his insistence though I did not progress beyond the first reader or so—that would have been when I was seven or eight. When I was thirteen in the Tenth Standard in Simla, the school found I would not be able to do the Punjab matriculation exam as I was under age. Appa explored various alternatives with his customary thoroughness and came up with the Calcutta Matric which I could take as a private student, studying at home. But I had to have a second language and Appa decided this would be Tamil, which I studied with the help of a friend of my parents. These Tamil lessons were quite impromptu as she had a brood of little ones who demanded her time and attention, so I learnt Tamil in between changing diapers or taking the second youngest out walking or getting ready a birthday party. But I did manage to scrape through and that was enough to inspire Appa; he suggested that I continue with Tamil as my second language for the Intermediate in college. That was in Madras, where standards were high and requirements tough—large swatches of poetry from Tamil classics and essays that were quite above my head. It was a daunting battle but I couldn't let him down, so I persevered and won. It gave me a smattering of knowledge of Tamil literature and a love for the language.

Yes, Appa opened up so much for me. Many years later when the anti-Hindi agitation in Madras aroused violent emotions and climaxed in several cases of self-immolation, Appa and I discussed the hold of language on people. Could it be so strong that young people were willing to sacrifice their lives for it? Appa recalled the love of the Hungarians for the Magyar language, the feelings of repression that led to the break-up of the old order and the emergence of nation-states in Europe. He talked of social violence, of the death wish and the parallels between fasts unto death and self-immolation. Appa had this great sense of history and a wonderful perspective, he could find incidents from the past and relate them to what was happening around you in the most fascinating way. Arising out of this we collaborated on an article in which we explored the sentiments of the Tamil people and the tremendous emotional hold of the language. I was delighted, and so was he, to see our names together when it was published in *Quest* the following year.

Appa's interests were diverse. He started to learn Sanskrit when he was fifty-three, the year my son—his first grandchild—was born. A year-and-a-half later when my second son was born, he was reading Kalidasa's *Raghuvamsa* and asked that the child be named Dilip. He was delighted that I chose David as Dilip's second name, and it tickled him that the lineage of the great Jewish poet-king should mingle with that of the epic Hindu heroic king in the names of his grandson. Appa had a deep interest in religions, had studied Judaism and Christianity in some depth and had explored a great deal of Hindu philosophy. He was always surprising you with his reading. I had vague memories of theories linking Jesus to Herod and the practice of killing new born baby boys as prevalent in several cultures, and never could remember where I had picked them up. Years later I read Robert Graves' *King Jesus* and started to tell him about it and found that he had read it when it was first published—it was proscribed, I think, and rather rare to find—and had apparently recounted it to me, so it lingered in the recesses of my memory. While studying in America I came across Radclyffe Hall's *The Well of Loneliness*, one of the first accounts, perhaps, of what life is like for a lesbian. Later in Madras I told Appa how moved I was by her account and was astonished to find he had read it in his university days soon after it was published. He spoke with sympathy about Radclyffe Hall, how she had faced great hostility and ostracism, and of her absolute personal integrity.

In South India surnames are not used, and men and women use the initials of their father's name or that of their village or family before their own name. Appa departed from this practice—was it vanity?—and made his name our surname. My brother's sons ensure that it will carry through to the fourth generation. Like most Indian men he had an undoubted preference for his only son. My brother, oldest of us four siblings, had a special place in the family. I was resentful of it at times, and it took long years to understand the Hindu psyche, which places so much emphasis on the male lineage. Appa could not free himself entirely from that. It did not stop him from giving his daughters the same opportunities for education, and he was proud of their accomplishments: my younger sister established a successful legal practice in Madras and the youngest got a doctorate in economics from the Sorbonne.

Though he didn't talk about his past, my father was very conscious of all that he had gone through and insisted that we work steadily at our books. He wanted his children to distinguish themselves academically, could be exacting and stern when results did not come up to his expectations and was equally pleased at marks of prowess. 'Life is a challenge,' he would often say, 'take up the challenge and do well.'

Going back in time to the Simla years I am once again reminded of the wonderful companionship he provided his daughter. He had a zeal and enthusiasm that was infectious. It was our first winter in Simla and it makes me smile even now to remember the insistent tapping on my door at midnight as he excitedly urged me to come out and we watched the snow work its quiet magic on the hillsides. He didn't want me to miss out on that first snowfall. There was the time when we trudged a good three miles, wearing overcoats and mufflers against the winter wind to attend Christmas Eve midnight service in the cathedral. I was thirteen and it seemed quite in the nature of things to make the effort to attend a Catholic mass though we did not belong to the faith. Appa wanted me to experience the wonder of that special service as much as he had wanted me to get to know Ibsen, and took me to the Gaiety Theatre on the Mall to see a performance of *The Doll's House*. We listened to the radio together the day Mahatma Gandhi was killed, the significance of the event etched in my fourteen-year-old mind by Appa's tears as he wept at the moving tributes paid by Pandit Nehru and Sarojini Naidu.

In those growing-up years the subject of caste never came up, it did not figure in our scheme of things, and I thought with naivete (that's hindsight speaking) that the caste system belonged to history. That is, until I went to college in Madras and lived in a hostel where I was asked what caste I was. The truthful, 'I don't know', met with disbelief. The assumption was that I was hiding something—or, was I teasing? Perhaps it was difficult to place me, my parents were in Delhi, my Tamil was accented. At home for the holidays, I questioned my father and he gave me a name which answered future questions from the girls in the hostel, though I didn't know any more about the caste than that. It was much later that I explored this area. Appa had made caste irrelevant and of no consequence to us and the knowledge that we belonged to a 'most backward' caste gave rise to much hilarity in family talk around the table.

When I finished university Appa did not mention marriage. We discussed job possibilities and knowing that I wanted to write or work on a newspaper, he steered me in that direction. This was unusual as parents of girls my age were busy scouting around for suitable husbands for their daughters. My decision to marry a Christian, across confines of region, language and religion evoked initial protest. He had not expected quite such a radical step from his eldest daughter. As I was in the USA, we exchanged a long series of letters discussing the implications of an inter-religious marriage. Appa and my husband got along well and all our apprehensions of a Hindu-Christian marriage turned out to be quite unfounded. Somewhere within him, though, Appa had hoped I would follow his example and opt for a career in the civil service rather than marriage. 'You settled for second best,' he said half in jest and half ruefully, 'you married into the civil service.'

There was hardly any open or physical demonstration of affection in the family, for all our 'westernization'. And yet one was wrapped in an aura of nurturing care and love and security. The night I went to the hospital for the birth of my first child, Appa placed his hand in blessing on my head and put a *tilak* on my forehead—the memory is very real and poignant even now, forty years later. After marriage in 1956 I made my home in Bombay but remained in close touch with Appa. We exchanged letters regularly and he was always there for advice or help when I needed it.

My first two children were born in Madras and all three went there every summer or Christmas to spend their holidays with their grandparents—a treat they greatly looked forward to. Appa had a very special relationship with his grandchildren, who adored and looked up to him. Sternness had been transmuted to gentle authority over the generation between and he could be firm and keep them in line without clashes or resentment. He admired, encouraged and praised his grandchildren, showered them with affection and glowed in their success. I wish we had been as fortunate, I thought wryly at times, we siblings had no rapport with our grandparents.

My mother was probably about sixteen when they married. She was a village girl with just about no schooling; in her first days at school, struggling with the alphabet she resented the encouraging slap administered by the teacher and decided she had had enough. After that she spent her days more usefully and pleasurably grazing the family cattle and swimming in the village stream. Marriage transplanted her from rustic Sundarapandiapuram, not even a dot on the map, to suburban Matunga in Bombay where Appa was a young officer in the Customs. She was very much a part of his social life as he was gregarious by nature and had a large circle of friends.

She spoke her own brand of Hindi, perfected over the years in Bombay, Calcutta and North India, and knew a few words of English. Appa taught her to read and write in Tamil and brought her magazines which she would read, slowly mouthing the words to herself. I have a picture of her in my mind that I treasure, one hand patting my infant daughter—named after her—to sleep, while she read the *Ramayana* held in the other.

My father was always solicitous of her. I often think about their relationship, turning over little nuggets of memory; Appa taking us for a drive to the Victoria Memorial in Calcutta, the four of us strolling along and stopping for a Magnolia ice-cream. That was a treat and for mother there was a chocolate-covered bar, a little more expensive and fancy than the ice-cream sticks he got for my brother and me. Mother was special, that was clear to my seven-year-old mind. And then, his voice calling out to her, 'Meenakshi!' as he opened the door coming home from work in the evenings.

She was deeply religious in a very private way. Pujas were not required of us, her fast days were for herself. Father scoffed at her observances, claiming that he himself was rational. Occasionally he would trip up, like the time he said that several astrologers had predicted that I, his eldest daughter, would have a *mlechha* marriage. I took him up on this count. 'I thought you didn't believe in astrologers,' I challenged. 'And then if you were told and presumably believed your daughter would marry a *mlechha*, why didn't you accept the inevitable, why did you protest?' That got a good-natured laugh and he tied himself up in knots trying to explain.

As he grew older he seemed to need religion on an emotional level; on the rational or intellectual level he rejected it and could not make that blind leap of faith to accept it unquestioningly. That didn't prevent him from the study of religion. When he was eighty and largely confined to the house because of hardening arteries and consequent inability to walk, he planned an essay competition and chose the subject: The Concept of the Messiah in Christianity and Hinduism. He hoped to make this a yearly affair and was disappointed at the indifferent response though he had offered a handsome prize. He began reading the Koran in a Tamil translation and was drawn to its ideas and language. He gave me an enthusiastic account of his progress but on my next visit to Madras to see him, said sadly that he had to give it up as his ability to concentrate and absorb was fast diminishing.

When he retired after all the active years in government service in Bombay and Calcutta, he chose to establish roots in Madras, and my parents and sisters lived there from 1955. The move to South India brought quite a change in Appa's life as it drew him into the affairs of his community. The Vanniyars had been organizing themselves to bargain with the government; they were looking for guidance as they aspired towards political clout and knew that with their force of numbers they could exert pressure as a group. Appa was well known in the community for his successes in the civil service, and he took on the role of mentor and adviser. He was glad to see this community of 'havenots', as he had described them to us, awakening politically, and he counselled them on strategy and sharpened their manoeuvring skills. As the years went by, he became a respected elder of the community, the patriarchal figure whose advice and money were sought by political aspirants as well as distant relatives, so that there were always supplicants of one sort or another on his front verandah. This disturbed, even dismayed me for his personality seemed to have changed ever so subtly. Did he enjoy all this? Was Appa succumbing to the feudal atmosphere that was still strong in Madras? It was a reversal of roles for the adolescent who had waited on another doorstep in Shencottah a generation ago.

Though he had long retired, the Tamil Nadu government asked him to head various commissions. In 1969 he was appointed chairman of the Backward Classes Commission to enquire into the condition of the backward classes in the state. The Report broke new ground and gave him a lot of satisfaction; there are passages in it that are Appa speaking out in his forthright manner, like a commentary on his own life:

> A Most Backward Class or even Scheduled Caste family with one or at the most two generations of affluence and public or Government service should not normally stand in need of any further favours from Government. If this does not happen, the first generation must be deemed to have failed in its duty to their own children and society, at whose cost aid was given to them. This must be admitted by the more fortunate sections of their castes and they must play their role in creating the proper environment for their children. Modern society and modern scholarship will not admit that there can be any environmental or social handicap which cannot be remedied in a generation of conscious effort, taking advantage of all the general advancement in education, science and technology . . . the forward castes should remember that our social institutions and traditions are responsible for large sections of the population remaining backward. In feudal and medieval society, inequality was regarded as essential for cultural development. Ancient civilizations were possible only because of slave and serf labour. A leisure class was maintained at the expense of a larger class of toilers. Such societies tumbled down largely because of this weakness. Modern democratic society is built on the concept of equality of opportunity. The cost involved in providing these equal opportunities must be treated as a

first charge on the State; and contributing to this cost should be viewed as a moral and social obligation of the privileged and better-off sections of society, and not merely as a penalty for the social evils perpetuated for centuries, though in fact it may be so.

The years following were busy with an inquiry into the working of municipal corporations in the state and a good deal of writing in the nature of political commentary. The University of Madras recognized his scholarship and understanding of socio-political trends when it invited him to deliver an endowment lecture in 1981 on the Dravidian Movement in South India. Our mother's death in 1985 desolated us all and left Appa very lonely, though he had three of his children around him. He looked forward as much as I did to my twice yearly visits to Madras, but something was happening to him, I couldn't quite understand. He disparaged displays of wealth and seemed disillusioned with material success. I puzzled over this, remembering my youthful accusations, remembering too his unabashed delight when my sister had confidently predicted that the bright young lawyer she was marrying would soon be earning a five-figure monthly income. His health was deteriorating steadily and with that he grew increasingly introspective. Brooding over his early years, he spoke bitterly of his father's greed and ambition driving him relentlessly through a childhood and adolescence deprived of even simple pleasures.

With grit and determination you can overcome anything, he had said. But Appa, you forgot to tell me that there are things in life that you cannot overcome, that you have to accept—as I learnt after headlong clashes with my eldest son. Ravi went through a troubled adolescence when he and I couldn't seem to agree on anything. His obstinacy was matched by my determination to force him around. Something had to give, and fortunately I had the sense to realize that I shouldn't persist, that I couldn't take the risk of breaking him and would have to take him as he was. It was a hard lesson, learnt the hard way. Through those trying, difficult years Appa had been steadfast in his faith in Ravi. In the late eighties, when Ravi chose to go into rural medical work rather than follow a profitable medical career in a city, Appa was happy and supportive. You could hear the pride in his voice when he spoke of his grandson's commitment.

Appa's life was a tribute to his courage and indomitable spirit. Perhaps, that was what made it hard for him to accept the infirmities and limitations of age. He raged at it, at the dying of the light as his diminishing eyesight curtailed reading and writing, he would not go gentle into the good night. He fumbled for words in those last, very last months, impatient at himself when he couldn't articulate what he wanted to say. For me it was wrenching to see my father humbled by time. And yet, even when age had feebled his step, dimmed his eyesight and hearing, when he was tired of the business of living, I still needed his help, still wanted to use him as a sounding board, wanted him to listen to my troubles and be my tower of strength—selfish as only a daughter can be.

In April 1990 I hurried to Madras in response to a call from my sister that Appa was in a precarious state. I spent a quiet few days with him. Earlier leave-takings had been emotional, difficult for both of us. This time he was calm. 'You come like a ray of sunshine into the winter of my days,' he said when it was time for me to go. After a pause he added, 'I may not see you again.' Appa died in June that year.

The death of the second parent is a terrifying moment, you are abruptly faced with your own mortality and the feeling that you are alone. When Appa died I was acutely, painfully, aware that my support and strength had gone, that there was no one to turn to. And there was anguish at the realization that I no longer was a daughter. A friend called, for a few moments neither of us could speak. Then she said softly, her words echoing my thoughts, 'Who will cherish us now, who will care for us?'

NOTE
1. Carl Marzani, *The Education of a Reluctant Radical* (*Roman Childhood*, vol. 1) (New York : Topical Books, 1992).

Chapter Eight

Bringing Him into Focus
Rinki Bhattacharya

Every time I began this piece, I wrote more about Ma, myself, my sister or others—Baba was almost absent from the family portrait. I struggle to get past the last thirty-three years to a time when he was there—to find words, images to repossess the man, but quickly realize it is very difficult to do so. I can understand why. Earlier, I was a grieving child, desperate to come to terms with my father's death, seizing every opportunity to fill the gaping emotional vacuum. Today I am a different woman—alone, older, tougher, practical, dry-eyed, and perhaps, quite unsentimental. A few objects link us to our shared past: a blue and white porcelain bought from a cheap London store when the entire family first visited Europe; the high ceilinged Godiwala bungalow with its red-tiled flooring, but life has otherwise changed beyond belief. Relationships between siblings, with Ma, with the rest of the family have altered beyond recognition. Writing about Baba, I constantly come up against these boundaries. I have to remind myself of the change within us—understand my new 'non' status, from an adored daughter to that of a divorced woman.

One memory haunting me is Ma's cool, firm voice saying, 'Wait till I tell your father.' I recall Ma's expression vividly, her lips a tight thin line; more frightening, her eyes—revealing nothing. When Ma did that my life came to a grinding halt. She exercised total control over the household. I doubt if Baba was aware of his omnipotent image or whether this too was a secret deal between our parents. Baba was the *annadata* and therefore deputed to be the arbiter of our destinies. But I do not remember him asserting that position of authority. It seemed, however, more and more necessary for Ma to repeat the awesome, 'I'll tell your Baba' threat as we grew up. I remember being afraid I had let my parents down, particularly Baba. I loved him deeply, needed his appreciation, and wanted to be admired. I felt unbearably threatened, being a timid child. Unable to display my emotions publicly, I would go into the bathroom and have a good howl after these public exposures. Portraying my invisible father I am continuously filled by sounds and images from our childhood. I remember most vividly our noisy, overcrowded home, a two-storey structure on Sardar Shankar Road in south Calcutta. The house sprang up without warning from the footpath: almost immediately you were in the *boshbar ghar* (sitting room) and could hear loud voices excitedly discussing the day's headlines, politics or the price of hilsa fish.

Baba's family belonged to the pre-Partition generation of immigrants from *Purbo Bangla* (East Bengal in British India). My elder uncles, Baba's three brothers, had left their ancestral Suapur estate in Dhamrai Thana by 1929. Baba was a student then, in his second year at Dhaka's famous Jagganath College. My grandfather, the zamindar of Suapur, died after a brief illness in 1930, and the family was ruined: the estate *nayeb* (accountant) declared there was a huge debt that had not been settled, and grabbed the entire Suapur estate. Baba was barely in his early twenties. From all accounts, he lived in a world of his own: he liked to sketch, paint, play the violin or take part in the plays that were put up for Durga Puja. He did not know how to outwit the unscrupulous accountant and took the only escape route, leaving with his widowed mother and two younger brothers for Calcutta where my eldest uncle, Sudhir Chandra Roy lived, working at an ordinary job. Baba never recovered from this tragedy. The theme of the dispossessed haunted him, as can be seen in his films like *Do Bigha Zamin* and *Bandini*.

Despite the lack of space and meagre pay packets, there was no discontent amongst us five girls—two sisters and three cousins. Baba often gave us surprise treats like a Sunday dip in the children's pool at the famous lakes or took us out to eat. On Bijoya Dashami day he would open the hood of his German BMW and crawl along with the sea of humanity towards the river for the *bisarjan* or immersion of the image of Durga. Returning home, on many occasions I faked sleep. Baba would drive to the garage, a few blocks away, with me apparently fast asleep. I am not certain why I resorted to these tricks, perhaps to have Baba all to myself, the assurance of his physical presence. He carried me home all the way. Other than these simulated situations I don't remember a hug or an embrace from either of my parents.

Our south Calcutta neighborhood was quite middle class, except for the two renowned painters—Baroda and Sharoda Ukil—and a barrister. Film directors and stars were considered to be not celebrities but social outcasts. Though Baba's very first directorial debut, New Theatre's *Udayer Pathe*, blazed a new trend in cinema, it did not bring him star status. The down-to-earth Bengali residents of our neighborhood treated him on a par with the rest. I was afraid of the cinema hall where larger than life characters leapt about. Baba would smuggle me out of the theatre, often stumbling in the dark. Calmed in his serene presence, I ate an ice cream till the show ended. Some nights I awoke with acute pain in my thin legs and called out to Ma. It was Baba who answered, sat by the bed, gently pressing my calves. If I stirred, his voice sounded anxious: 'Is the pain less?' How often I saw his burning cigarette tip glow with each puff while Ma slept and the household rested, an image of reassurance to my wild childish imagination which saw eerie shapes in the dark. These wordless moments, discreet, unstated, nurtured our commitment to one another which lasted till the bittersweet end.

I had believed our seamless childhood—school, uneaten tiffins, home, games on the footpath, the excitement of Lakshmi Puja—would last lifelong. One day the entire Calcutta establishment folded up. The second-hand khaki army holdall was spread out like an ailing relative. Baskets, packages, shoes, clothes littered the house. Ma expertly handled this entire operation along with our cook, Mohan. I insisted that she pack our two kittens also. Baba said a sharp, 'No'. Unused to hearing him being so harsh, I resorted to crying. But the kittens were abandoned. This was my first row with Baba. I sulked on the train and did not speak to him. Those two nights and two days marked the longest journey in my life, tearing me apart between the two worlds of Calcutta and Bombay. I feel that parting ache even today, after more than forty years in Bombay, as did Baba, aching to return to his native village, even for a glimpse, before he died.

For Baba, the migration from New Theatres and Bengal left him with feelings of alienation that he never shared. Looking back I realize why he had withdrawn into himself, grown lonely. When we left Calcutta, it was as though a part of Baba stayed back. In our own way, each of us felt the wrench.

The most important event was kept a secret till Ma, who had been putting on weight, simply vanished one morning. We sisters were told she had gone to get our sister from the hospital. The house felt strange and empty without her and Baba stayed home longer. When I awoke, my first thought was of Ma's absence but then I remembered with some relief that Baba was home. I went through one empty room to another till I reached the verandah at the back. Baba was slouched in an easy chair, I couldn't recall seeing him so defenceless. I stood on the threshold, behind the curtains, fearful of making a sound. Several minutes passed. 'Khuki,' Baba called out. I emerged, not knowing how to start a conversation with him. 'Khuki,' Baba repeated, ruminating, 'how does your Ma make stew?'

The arrival of our sister, born during the very first monsoon in Bombay, signified a new phase in my relationship to Baba. I became a woman at ten. Baba's praise was expressed in grunts or positive body language, unlike Ma, who was well versed in language whether in praise or criticism. The ambience at home was generally appreciative. Once the desire to play the piano obsessed me. A teacher, Miss Chenoy, was found and within a week she found a suitable upright piano for sale. I nagged Baba day and night, and he went along with a small delegation that included my enthusiastic music teacher. The piano was bought for a whopping two thousand five hundred rupees. In later years, when studies engrossed me, and I neglected music, the expensive piano was little more than an obsolete toy. Baba did not resent that I had made him part with such a large sum for it.

Watching my parents interact, their affectionate, sensitive scrutiny of each other, filled me with a sense of tranquil security. I was careful to display no partisan feeling. Both Baba and Ma had to be on my side, and I assumed that they were. Children the world over share a universal guilt of 'growing up', some of us feel more guilty than others. I was twice guilty. I grew up without either of my parents noticing, nor did they suspect I was falling in love.

Basu was no stranger to our large, comfortable home. He was employed briefly as Baba's assistant. Returning from school, once my attention was caught by his loud rendition of a Bengali poem to an attentive Ma. His closeness to Ma provided a source of great reassurance. I took this as conclusive proof of her consent. I blindly believed Basu, who said that all was well, that together we would break the news to my parents and receive their blessings.

Ma caught us together in a clandestine meeting foolishly held in the neighbouring Mount Mary's Church. Led back home, I was to be the prime eyewitness to my own downfall that evening. In a total daze, I heard Ma mutter those dreaded words: 'Wait till your Baba returns,' before collapsing on the bed. Neighbours were summoned and everyone ran around as in an emergency. I retreated to the tiny unlit study behind the main house.

When Baba returned home, Ma was in bed, watched over by our neighbours and my sister Tatu. When I crept in I saw that Baba had his back to me. He turned abruptly. For a split second his gaze strayed over me. Silently he proceeded towards the door. At the threshold he stopped. 'If . . . if . . . if . . . you . . . ever . . . meet . . . that . . . I . . . will . . . disown . . . you.' His words shot past me, the voice, his delivery, did not belong to him. Moreover, this was the longest sentence I remember from Baba to me or anyone. What struck me at once was the ominous sounding new word—'disown' in Bengali. I did not know what it meant. His forbidding tone was enough. I stood rooted to the spot. After weeks and months of relentless torment, that included a failed suicide attempt on my part, Basu and I eloped and were married in secret. Later in September, when our son, Aditya, was born, I insisted on Ma being present at the maternity home. She came, still angry and unforgiving.

In retrospect, I realize that concealing my affair with Basu from Baba damaged our relationships beyond repair. Not only between me and Ma or Baba, but with all my three siblings who now had a distorted image of me, perceiving me as the harbinger of destruction—a perception even imposed unjustly on my children. Our few peace overtures met with disastrous results. Ma demolished them with chilling certainty: 'Her father will never forgive Rinki!' And yet it was this unforgiving, unbending father who, with quiet dignity, reclaimed me. It is his vision, understanding, kindness that transforms my ordinary story into one of rescue and regeneration.

One night the city was lashed by incessant rain, water flooded the area and almost reached our small ground floor apartment. Basu had left home before the deluge; till midnight there was no trace of him. I sat alone, my infant son on my lap, feeling very uneasy. By one or two o'clock in the morning paranoia gripped me and I woke up our kind landlady. She rang up my parents with whom I had had no further contact. Within minutes Baba's car and driver were at our door awaiting orders. When we ran short of money for the house deposit, it was Baba who stepped in, though we still hadn't been formally accepted by the family. On the day that Ma longed to see her grandson and secretly had us over, Baba returned home, unexpectedly, at noon. He picked up my son, ignorant of the child's identity, and walked into the bedroom. Ma nervously began to prepare a *paan* and I didn't know where to hide. Baba didn't react at all. 'How are you, Khuku?' he asked, in his calm voice, as though nothing was wrong. He remembered to ask about Basu. The myth about Baba's wrath was already crumbling. It was Baba who made the first truly statesmanlike gesture with grace and humility, in accepting Basu as his son-in-law.

In the autumn of 1965, Baba was dying. He was being treated at the Tata Memorial Hospital for cancer. He had returned from England after British specialists advised Ma that it was time for him to be with the family. I was in the seventh month of a second pregnancy. A few months before Baba's death a Pune *vaidya*, who claimed to achieve miracles, emerged on the scene. That's what we wanted—a miracle to save Baba. The *vaidya* ordered Baba to move to Pune and we did so. From then onwards, everything happened all too soon. As the baby grew in my womb, Baba's life ebbed; he was past hope and soon we realized that though the *vaidya* took large sums of money, there would be no miracle. Baba and I lived with our unsaid feelings, we did not need words. There was no barrier between us. In my helpless state, the baby due soon, all I could do was sit by him, touch his throbbing forehead, his aching legs. That is all I did, remembering gratefully Baba's nocturnal vigils over me when as a little girl, I felt his healing touch. At these times, discreetly, we defeated death, triumphed over all feeling of loss, pain, anger, bitterness. From the autumn of 1965 I was continuously with my parents despite Ma's protests. Irritable and worn out, Ma sometimes scolded me, said harsh words, asked me to leave. After she left the room, Baba would break down crying, 'Don't go away—Khuku—don't leave me alone—' I could not leave. Silently I would nod, acquiesce, my fingers pressing his forehead quickened their pace.

I delivered prematurely, three weeks ahead of the doctor's calculations. I remember clearly the evening I returned from the nursing home. Baba was sitting outdoors in the pale retreating sunlight; he looked grey, withered. I took the baby to him. He touched her forehead gently, said something inaudible. It was New Year's Eve. We held a festive homecoming of sorts, got Baba's favourite Chinese food, tried to cheer him, coax him from his painful enclosure—but Baba had already withdrawn from life. When I began this piece, I wrote that I cannot find Baba in our animated family portrait nor can I find myself. But every time I return home, no matter what day or time, I neatly push my slippers under the rack, keep my bag in place, tidy tables, papers, put fresh flowers in a bowl—I am startled by the strange likeness of our beings. That defiant spiritual bond between us stubbornly keeps me going, moving beyond each struggle, a bond that continues to inspire me.

Chapter Nine

My Invaluable Mentor
Priti T. Desai

A dark, broad-framed, beer-bellied man with black curly hair, sleepy eyes, reserved, introverted, that was Pappa, a man of few words, a presence hard to ignore, intelligent, prodigiously hard-working with a driving ambition. He had an infallible memory, photographic they used to say. He appeared and was haughty and arrogant, though surprisingly well loved by most of his friends and those who worked with him.

The eldest of five siblings—four daughters and a son—I had been the only child till I was five and a half. Our bond was nourished when as a child he treated me as an equal. I recall our Sunday jaunts to shops for toys, books, records and visits to museums or the zoo. Occasionally it would be a morning lazily spent in an Irani cafe where I ate toast oozing with butter and then revelled in drinking what was described on their blackboard as a milk-colddrink, while he studied the racing handicaps. Sometimes I accompanied him to his deserted office on a Sunday morning to quietly day dream ; at other times it was to meet his film producer friend visiting from Lahore. I just tagged along in his adult world. Playing cricket in the garden, flying kites during the winter, learning to spin tops, being initiated into playing cards—yes, he was my playmate too.

He spoilt me, yet he disciplined me in an unusual way. He rarely raised his voice or hand, the look in his eyes was cue enough. Most of my requests were met, a few refused. I had taken a fancy for a cheap flute but Pappa refused to buy it so the next day I bought it with the help of the cook. That evening, he was livid and hit me once with the flute and promptly threw it in the back alley. That was the only physical reprimand at his hands. Thereafter I learnt not to ignore his wishes.

He was a friend and companion sorely missed when he was away for months in Africa on business trips. Pappa's friends still tease me over the way I howled and wept, aged three, when he left for Mombasa. Mummy and I were at the pier to bid him goodbye. He boarded the ship and I saw the gangway slowly drawn away. How would he get off the ship? Would he not fall into the sea? My fears and tears intermingled. The stuffed tortoise and the beads he brought me from Africa were for long my favourites.

An often repeated story of his childhood now seems revealing. My grandfather, Bapa, was stationed in a small town in Gujarat and Pappa was sent to school. The master defending the old axiom 'spare the rod and spoil the child' (charmingly rendered in Gujarati as *'soti vage chum chum ne vidya aave ram zham'*—the whizzing cane hits and knowledge hastens) made him miserable. He found an original way to dodge this. He left at the normal time for school, found a cosy ledge near a tailor's shop on the way, settled down and slept, returning home in the late afternoon. After a few days Bapa took him to the tailor for his clothes. 'Oh, so this is your son? I see him sleeping on the ledge here every day!' His escapade was over. He explained the reason for his truancy and was then sent to a madrasa. Perhaps, that was why he accepted my reluctance as a child to attend a regular school. I went to the Montessori class in a neighbourhood school. A favourite uncle came for a holiday and his stories of distant forests, *shikars*, maharajas were far more fascinating than the routine of school. I did not wish to go to school and my parents allowed me to stay at home during his visit. Once my uncle left, I told Pappa that I did not like going to school and he arranged for a tutor to come in the mornings for three hours and I studied at home till the Fourth Standard.

The afternoons were my own—to read, to play, to indulge in eating savouries without restraint. As I grew older, he encouraged me to browse, buy and read books. The only time Pappa, one of the most liberal men I knew, restricted me was when he put away Henry Miller's *Tropic of Cancer* and D. H. Lawrence's *Lady Chatterley's Lover* (both proscribed then) when I was fifteen, and said I could read them when I was older. I did not take this amiss.

How book-oriented Pappa was! The written word was most trusted: a very Brahmin trait. I had little idea of my biological self when faced with menstruation at the age of ten. I was oblivious of the fact that I was a woman now, no longer a child. My adolescent tantrums could not be tackled by Mummy as she was unable to explain this natural process of growing up. Pappa tried to remedy this by promptly giving me the book *Grow Up and Live*; ironic that I read it too late, my English was not up to it then.

For me he was a guru, though I discovered it very late. As a girl of nine, he had me marching with the allied troops in Europe: we followed the movements on each front as we marked the map every morning, listening to BBC. Later we read biographies of Hitler and Mussolini. When European and Far Eastern business friends visited us in postwar years, talks inevitably led to their personal experiences during the Second World War. In the changing world, nationalization and planning became part of economic policy. This meant we read corporate history, political theory. An eye-opening education indeed.

Pappa's younger sister was a brilliant student and had death not snatched her away when she was studying for her B.A. in the late twenties, she would have been the first woman graduate in our community. I was told Pappa was deeply attached to her and this bond may have led to his strong faith in education, especially for women. Was I replacing this lost sister? Yet I think education to him was more an accomplishment than a preparation for a career. But with changing times when my younger sisters went to university a decade later, he wanted them to take courses that would help them pursue independent professions.

His two-year stay in England where he was sent for training during 1929-1931 influenced him in many ways. As a child, apart from dresses, I wore shorts and skirts, my ears were not pierced and at his insistence my hair was kept short. Indeed I had to beg to be allowed to grow my hair so I could wear flowers in my plaits. I called my parents 'Pappa' and 'Mummy', a sure sign of British influence. Was I a brown saheb's child? The son he wanted?

When I turned eighteen he laid down two rules for me; one, that I was not to smoke. The other, I was not to cut my hair short! Did he now see me as an Indian woman or was it that this reflected his subconscious love for Mummy who had very long and lustrous hair or did his current mistress have long hair? These rules were easy to keep. He gave me freedom and choice and the responsibility it entailed. I did not realize that he had given me the gift of independence and I had to formulate my own rules. Pappa never queried me about my friends, my outings, my holidays, my spending, even my first ordering a beer in his presence in Sri Lanka did not make him bat an eyelid!

My efforts to look pretty with a layer of Cuticura talcum powder on my face, he would wipe off with his hanky. Was it that my already fair skin needed no such adorning or was he reminded of a tart? His injunction was not to wander under the noon day sun when I visited my granny for that would darken my skin. Year after year, on Naraka Chaturdashi, the day prior to Diwali, he narrated the story of how children who did not wake up to have a ritual bath before sunrise would turn the colour of a crow. 'How do you know,' I asked him. Pappa explained that he had slept too late and had turned black—my childish mind accepted this story of how my fair father turned dark. Was he colour conscious, I wonder?

For him, knowledge, rationality, honesty, sincerity and integrity had far greater value than possessions. I was not chastised for accidentally breaking a valued bottle of cognac, only a gentle concern that I might have hurt myself. In the forties the flat metal box that held fifty cigarettes was highly prized as a pencil box at school. Pappa, a chain-smoker, got those and I hoarded them and occasionally would part with them to school friends whose fathers did not smoke. One Sunday morning the dhobi asked me for a box and I told him I had none to spare. Maybe Pappa overheard me. For the next week no empty box came my way; although I saw Pappa putting away five of them on top of his wardrobe. Next week when the dhobi arrived Pappa gave him all the boxes and I got a curt look. Possessions were for sharing, whether it was a heavy winter coat, expensive leather cabin trunks, or a pocket watch. He could give with graciousness, never with a thought of any return. His innate trust in humans meant nothing was locked in our house—one was never saddled with keys. His philosophy was that he earned by the sweat of his brow, and fruits of honesty are never stolen, and this still holds true for us.

Pappa was a man of strong contradictions. Rooted in the land where he was born, he made us aware of our heritage. We went for midnight *darshan* of Krishna on Janmashtami and followed the Govinda processions where people danced, forming human pyramids to break the pots hung high. For us the Ganesha festival began by viewing the small idols fetched by families from the window of his school friend's chawl room in Girgaon, followed by the finale of man-sized idols immersed at Chowpatty Beach. Another annual event was the visit to the traditional Gujarati theatre at Bhangwadi. The family drama with tragic overtones was set off by enough comic interludes, and was interspersed with songs that had as many encores as the audience demanded by their lusty loud clapping. We all inherited his love for the theatre. He loved the monsoon magic of wild waves and green hues of the countryside. He would ask Mummy to take a drive along the seafront to see the waves when he came home for lunch; he took us all for long drives in the Ghats on Sundays during the monsoon. Later, when paralysis made him homebound I often saw him watching the heavy pelting raindrops as he sat on his swing—the windows wide open for him to savour the rains.

His love for cricket, football, tennis, hockey, horse racing meant an early initiation for us as well. The dandy clothes—three-piece suits, garters, suspenders, dinner jacket with stiff front shirts; the bows, the ties, the watch, the cuff links. His habits—chain-smoker, fondness for beer, whisky, steak, chicken and French cuisine. He was saheb enough in his couture, hobbies and ideas but retained a middle class life-style.

From his puritan father he had learnt some bitter lessons which he chose not to inflict on his own children. He had no inhibitions and retained his naturalness with us. Having been mercilessly beaten by his father for the sin of eating *paan*, he introduced his children to 'bad' habits early enough. He disowned his father's belief, not by open rebellion or even direct confrontation; just silently, by doing what he pleased. His schoolmaster father had a hard life and prized thrift; not so Pappa, who spent on cigarettes, clothes, toys, betted at the race course, rented a large house in a comfortable bourgeois locality with servant and cook thrown in.

My idyllic childhood was nevertheless tinged with traumas that made the transition to teenage difficult. The night my baby sister, Kalindi, was seriously ill, Pappa was not at home. Mummy woke up my grandpa when she saw Kalindi go into convulsions. Bapa immediately rushed to call the doctor. It was too late. When Pappa returned she was breathing her last. Mummy was in a state of shock. I had lost a long awaited playmate. I felt a vague uneasiness. Over the years I remember Pappa would always hurry out after dinner and return late in the night. Soon he became scarce on Sunday afternoons too. I was nine years old when one night I woke up to a loud cry from Mummy and I heard knocks on our bedroom door. Mummy had tried to drink poison because she could not bear the mental torture any longer—she was accused of infidelities by my father. That night I saw my father as someone evil and from then on, I hated my mother's husband. I always had a lurking distrust of him. What I could not fathom was how these unhappy parents of mine continued to breed more children. To me, this loveless relationship with its haunting silences and lack of communication was incompatible with an increasing family. It soured my mind, and I now distrusted men and the idea of becoming a wife did not attract me. In later years I felt a raging, seething anger at the helplessness of women without economic independence. Was I intending to fight the battle that my mother had lost?

One day, when I was nineteen, Pappa wanted me to accompany him to a millionaire's wedding. Mummy had refused to go as she found the crowd snobbish. She suggested that if I chose to go, I should ask my father to get the jewellery from the bank vault. Jewels, she insisted, were very necessary for the occasion. Pappa did not fetch the jewel box. Seeing that I was in no mood to get dressed, he sensed something was afoot. When I told him that I would not attend weddings without wearing some jewels, he was rather vocal for a father who rarely talked except in monosyllables. He said that he would not take his daughter if she believed she was valued for her jewels. 'People value you for what you are and not for your dress and jewels or what you possess.' It was a lesson well learnt: my guiding principle in forming relationships has been to value persons for what they are, rather than their status or possessions.

Within his family ran a thread of insanity. Pappa's paternal uncle had been a brilliant student and had gone to study in London at the beginning of this century. He had a nervous breakdown and returned insane. One of Pappa's older brothers could not keep pace with my father's academic brilliance. This uncle simply gave up and lingered on: healthy, clean in his habits and attire, he rarely talked but was intelligent enough to read the *Times of India*. He lived in the country with another brother, visited the railway station morning and evening, and it was said the trees bore testimony to his rounds as most of the soft bark was chewed by him as also the edges of the wooden swing at home—a favourite seat of the Desai family.

Pappa's father, Bapa, arranged for his first grandchild's marriage. At the beginning of the Second World War, his grandson-in-law was arrested for suspected leftist leanings under the dreaded Defence of India Rules. My distraught aunt made Bapa feel guilty though he and Pappa did manage the grandson-in-law's release. The worry, sleeplessness, and enormous stress broke Bapa and he became insane. Pappa took care of his father; I recall how the windows were papered over to comply with the blackout restrictions during the war and whenever there was any slight stirring at night Pappa would awaken, switch on the lights and rush to Bapa's bedroom. Kerosene stove and matches were now kept in the servants' quarters—no suicidal material was left around the house. Bapa recovered a little and wishing to leave Bombay, moved to a small town where Kaka lived. Maybe depression once again engulfed him. Bapa was left alone in a room and locked up; one night he hanged himself. Pappa must have found this very traumatic, yet I do not recall him ever talking about Bapa's death.

At significant milestones like when I finished school, turned eighteen or on their twenty-fifth wedding anniversary, Pappa would speak of sending me for postgraduate studies to Cambridge. Was this an excolonial's idea of power through knowledge or was it pure fantasy? To me it was a precious promise. I got my master's in economics and thought my next move would be to Cambridge as I had excellent marks. He evaded the question. That day I realized he was not going to keep his promise. I felt betrayed. If he had owned up to his lack of resources, I would have understood. Or when I started college and he despaired that I was not working half as hard as he did, he could have warned me that academic excellence was necessary to win a competitive scholarship. A German business friend made an offer that I could go to Munich, stay with his family and learn languages. Pappa pooh-poohed the idea. He later mumbled, 'You don't understand. I would have to pay a price for that and I'm not willing to be bought.'

I went into a severe depression, my sense of worthlessness was overwhelming and I lost hope. I withdrew into myself, into silence, staring out of my bedroom window, refusing to leave my room. Pappa was deeply disturbed. Did he see a repetition of his family history? A few weeks later he had a massive stroke. It was a hard blow for us all. Overnight our lives changed. A sense of guilt haunted me. Had he been so worried about me that it led to this? With the right side of his body paralysed, he lay helpless, his eyes looking for support. I told myself that I would stand by him my father, my friend. I was twenty-one, he was barely fifty-one.

The last sixteen years of his life is another story. He battled paralysis with tenacity. His tremendous will power, obstinacy and determination made it possible for him to piece his life together again. He rarely complained about his physical limitations. Soon he adjusted to reality—from a chauffeur-driven car to public buses to being home-bound; listening to BBC for interest and AIR during the day to kill time. He took an interest in his children's activities and their friends. He was no lover of music, yet would tune in to Begum Akhtar at full volume so that I could enjoy it in another room. He travelled when he could. Once when our neighbour's son was howling Pappa asked me to investigate. The boy had been restrained from sprinkling talcum powder on the bedroom floor in play—the reason for his tears. Pappa suggested I call the boy over and allow him to play with the powder in our home. The neighbourhood children loved him. He would entertain their whims and fancies and they would confide their fears for which simple remedies were offered. Nightmares were contained by feet being washed before going to bed.

As his outside world diminished, he enjoyed watching from the sidelines. A cricket test match at the Brabourne Stadium and Pappa insisted on our buying a ticket so that one of us could watch it live. When friends rang up for race tips, he was always ready, having studied the form, the pedigree, in great detail. With his left hand he still wrote his racing notes. When the Oaks, Derby, St. Leger were run at Mahalaxmi Race Course, he would goad Mummy or a sibling to go. Years later I was amazed and amused when I was in England and found that my cousin was perturbed that our reunion could not include a trip to the Newmarket races, and an English friend was upset that he could not take me to Epsom. Well, I bid farewell to racing once Pappa passed away. Yet how deeply the habit was imprinted—I still reckon the first Thursday of June as Derby day at Epsom!

An arranged marriage with a girl of fifteen (when he was twenty-two) and his insistence that his wife attend school after she was married, seems strange. For a village-bred girl, my mother must have found the tempo of life in the metropolitan city rather unnerving. At school as the only married student Mummy must have felt awkward, especially when Pappa was away in England for two years and her friends could not fathom the restrictions placed on her by her in-laws. Mummy had to fend for herself. I do not think Pappa ever was aware of her traumas. Hindu families (more so amongst Anavil Brahmins), viewed daughters as *saap no bhar* (a serpent's burden). During my teenage years when I vacationed with my mother's family I could not fathom their barbed comments. 'Your father would have to beg from house to house to find a husband for you', 'You will be thrown out by your in-laws,' 'With an upbringing like yours, you will not last long anywhere.' As I grew older I avoided visiting relatives. I decided Pappa would not be servile for his daughter's sake—mates could be found in other ways. A Hindu girl from birth is conditioned to believe that being a *pativrata* woman is her highest ideal. Yet Pappa chose to bring me up not to become a servile wife but an individual in my own right. I was encouraged to have an open questioning mind, I had to find my own answers. Mummy later revealed that in my upbringing he was deeply influenced by Bertrand Russell's ideas. There was never a reference, even oblique, to marriage as I entered my teens. When I told him of a girl from my college being very unhappy in her husband's home, he told me never to have fears on that score. If I were ever unhappy, his doors would always be open to me. This was extremely humane and modern for a Hindu father, for, traditionally, once the daughter was married off, his role in her life was minimal. Now I wonder whether this was his way of atoning for his own behaviour towards his wife.

Never was there any hint that being a daughter I had gender-related status. Even after our only brother was born, he did not make any distinctions amongst us. No preference was shown to his son. He did not demand obedience and respect. He got what was his due. Nevertheless, his male dominance was very real to my mother.

The reality of being a woman crushed me when aged twenty-one, I was looking for a job. At interview after interview the answer was, 'No, since you are a woman. If you were a man, we would have no hesitation!' The woman in me was hurt. Deep within me was embedded my goal of being *pitasarkhi, putra samovadi* (like father, equal to a son).

A year after I received my masters degree, I took up a lectureship at the University of Delhi. Following premature retirement, Pappa was offered consultancy work by a Swiss company. This was my opportunity to stand by him—to prove that I was no less than a son. I left Delhi to assist Pappa, to be his right hand. Pappa insisted that I share part of his fees, ensuring that I was an economically independent daughter. A decade later when I had an immigration visa for Canada, he told me that I should be happy in what I did with my life. No pressure to stay and take care of an aging sick father. That I chose not to go was entirely my own decision.

More recently, when I was immobilized by a hip fracture, I recalled Pappa's continuous request, 'Make me comfortable', as he lay flat in bed after surgery on his fractured paralytic leg, with uncontrolled spasms shaking him. It took more than six months for him to be mobile again. My tribulations were just for three weeks, as aided by a walker and modern surgery I was soon on my feet. It was then that I understood that for Pappa his world had been shattered, his ambition unfulfilled, his job gone, robbed of sexual pleasure by his physical disability. It was a slow but certain submission of his will. Yet he kept his will and sanity intact, he chose patience with the outside world. When I walked out to resume work, it was his old stick that gave me confidence to face the future.

Pappa never advocated ties of language or community or caste, nor did he clutter my mind with prejudices, never talked disparagingly of any belief or religion. To all outward signs he was an agnostic. During Diwali when Mummy and I went to the temple, he never accompanied us, preferring to wait outside. When I questioned him on Islam he read to me Mohammed's biography. At times he quoted from the Bible. As a student at Wilson College, a Protestant institution in Bombay, he won a prize for scripture, which I was later to win too. The impact of his study of Christianity was his Christian spirit, a most precious legacy. He rarely spoke disparagingly of anyone, even those who had used him, maintaining that if you cannot speak good of someone, that is a flaw; the greater fault was to speak ill.

After he suffered the stroke which left his entire right side paralysed, he took a special trip to Mathura to fulfil a vow that our aged orthodox Vaishnav neighbour had made. He clambered up a flight of steep stairs, to attend a Satyanarayan Puja which an old neighbour of more than four decades had offered as a thanksgiving for Pappa's being able to walk again. During a visit to Calcutta he even accompanied Mummy to offer prayers at the Tarakeshwar temple. Mummy was devout, and her faith had seen her through the trying years of Pappa's sickness—perhaps he had grown to respect her need for a spiritual anchor.

He rarely talked about his experiences, though he had travelled all over India and the world. How I craved for his insights! I treasured the letters which he wrote once a week when he was abroad. He told us of his joy at finding a swing in the hotel at Venice and how he had almost swung all night! He described the chateaux de la Loire, the battleground of Waterloo, discovering a few cackling hens when he crossed beyond the Iron Curtain from Trieste. He wrote that the Quartier Latin in Paris had rowdy students, but acceded to my request and found me a Sorbonne student for a penfriend. He mentioned the plays he saw in London. Yet when he returned, any queries from us evoked only a 'yes' or a 'no'. What was he afraid of? Intimacy? Did he feel vulnerable? Pappa loved us, yet rarely confided in us. His silence, aloofness, lack of communication caused me acute pain. Was his silence a weapon to ward us off? Was it indifference or withdrawal?

Our home was open to relations and friends, just to stay, or come for medical treatment. He used to say, 'Since we have a home people come, if it was not there no one would turn up.' Mostly one inferred his ideas from the very few remarks he made. Whilst a number of his nephews lived with us, he showed them little affection, only a grudging and brusque acknowledgement of their presence. Yet he actively helped them to get jobs, a privilege he did not deem fit for me. Pappa never bragged about his achievements or talked about his compassionate acts, his personal relationships, his friends. He never referred to the help he had given, how much, to whom—there was no expectation of return favours. Once I recall he mumbled, 'You don't give so that you may receive in return; you give because you like it and you would be untrue to yourself if you did otherwise.'

Here was a man who consistently presented profits for his company; and yet when he took ill at the age of fifty-one, there was no balance in his bank account nor were there any investments. He had shockingly overreached himself, indulging in wine, women and song. When he was well and the breadwinner, he kept Mummy on a tight leash as his profligate spending reduced the household budget to the minimum. Once he suffered the stroke, the purse-strings were in Mummy's hands. She treated him with fairness and indulged him in his little pleasures, though with the expenses of university-going children it was impossible to meet all his whims. In the decade of his trial we became closer as a family.

While his expensive life-style could easily have made him corrupt, his corporate conscience was not swayed by easy money. During the Second World War a Marwari businessman sent a schoolfriend of Pappa's to pay him Rs 50,000 in cash if he would settle a claim in his favour. The friend was shown the door. The opportunities were immense, but he remained true to his father's principle: honesty above all else. Yet he was dishonest with Mummy. I was bewildered by these ethical opposites in Pappa's nature. He still remains an enigma.

His maniacal corporate loyalty I could neither understand nor respect. The company had given him the opportunity to develop and so he gave it his total loyalty. He never took a holiday, never took a day off, marched to work even after a 24-hour flight from London. For three decades he slaved on. An ego trip, a sense of power? Ultimately there was not even a farewell when he prematurely retired after his disabling stroke. He must have been deeply hurt, but concealed that pain within him till the last. Pappa was always happy and delighted when his juniors dropped in. He was lucky that his integrity was well respected and his Swiss business friends appointed him as a consultant, enabling him to live with dignity.

From my early, initial distrust of men as an adult I easily made male friends owing to a faith in humanity which Pappa had nurtured. Consequently, I have had strong platonic friendships, along with a distrust of sexual relationships—also a sign of coming to terms with my father. Yes, because of him, I could neither take men as protectors nor be intimidated by them. His silent approval allowed me to live my life my way. From a shy, reserved, introverted girl, I became a rational, confident, independent woman. It is strange that only now I understand that it was the boundless affection that he had given me that shaped and taught me to enjoy life. In later years his demands were few and he appeared self-absorbed. Ill health had marginalized him. Pappa may have felt hurt, for as years passed, we were more engrossed in our own lives. Sometimes when we overruled him, he used to mumble, 'When I'll no longer be here, then you will realize the value of this old man.' Now I see him as my invaluable mentor.

A few weeks before he passed away, I broached the subject of drawing up a will. 'You do it,' he said. I guess I had earned his trust. He taught me an unforgettable lesson jolting my materialistic mind. To commemorate their centenary the Swiss company had published a book, and Pappa and I had worked on some sections relating to the Indian subcontinent. As a memento the company presented a desk clock to Pappa. One afternoon the clock was missing—Mummy was asleep, Pappa was on his swing. I was angry that someone could walk away with this precious sentimental gift whilst both of them were home. I sulked and on the third day when he could bear it no longer, he said, 'Things can be replaced. What will you do when you lose someone you love?' Was there a message in this, I wonder, a distillation of his life's experience?

Chapter Ten

Que Sera Sera
Sarah Major

My father came out to India with the British army. He was the physical instructor of his regiment, the Yorks and Lancs, and served in many parts of the country. After his stint with the army ended, he decided to stay on and joined the Bombay City Police, at a time when all the officers were British. He met my mother in 1907 and they were married the same year. He grew to love India, my mother's country.

Born in 1875 in Derbyshire, in a small village called Stavely, he was one of thirteen children. His father worked as a millwright and his weekly packet had to stretch a long way. It was only when the children grew older and could take on jobs such as delivering newspapers or milk bottles before leaving for school or work, that life became comfortable. Their pleasures were simple and inexpensive like playing football or watching a game or going fishing. As a young boy my father longed to leave his little home town and see a bit of the world. He would confide in his mother and tell her he had two choices: the army or the navy. He was not too fond of the sea and it would mean long and dreary months on a ship with only the crew for company. On the other hand, The army offered the opportunity of meeting people and making many friends—and living in another country. When the chance arose he applied and was accepted and India, which had only been a dream, now became a reality.

My father met my mother in a most unusual way. A court case was being fought by the state for her brother who was a minor. My widowed grandmother, some years earlier, was the guardian of her young son's inheritance. While she was signing the papers for the interest on the securities that formed part of his inheritance, a young man happened to visit her; he offered to help her with the papers and save her the trouble. But he not only pocketed the interest but also sold the share certificates. My grandmother took the case to court and my father, now a police officer, was in charge of the case. He used to visit my grandmother often to discuss the matter and met and grew to like my mother. Shortly afterwards he proposed to her. The case had a happy ending as it was withdrawn when the young man's family not only returned the interest but also bought back the certificates and gave them to my grandmother. And my parents got married.

As far as I remember, my father never went back to visit England and later I learnt why. In 1913 he had a longing to see his mother and be with his brothers and sisters. Leaving my mother and three small children with her parents, he made the trip to England by himself. While he was away, both my older sisters fell badly ill with dysentery, the younger one recovered but my eldest sister died before my father's return. In those days ships from England took over a month to reach India, and it was only when my father arrived home that he learnt the sad news. He must have reproached himself for having been away, for he promised my mother that he would never leave us again. And he kept his word. Perhaps a memory of my father saying he would not leave India again registered in my subconscious somewhere. I don't know, but I never had the urge to leave India or go to England, whereas my sister and her family left in 1947 to make England their home. My mother spent two holidays with them, and on her third trip decided to stay on in England and she died there in 1972.

My father must have been deeply saddened by the loss of his eldest daughter. Later I sensed some of his anguish and heartfelt sorrow, which were expressed in the words engraved on her tombstone, *Que sera sera*, what will be will be. Many, many years later those words were made famous when Doris Day sang the song, and whenever I heard it I would remember my sister and how much my father must have missed her.

I remember a little incident when I was six years old and had a bad attack of whooping cough. I would cough and the whooping would go on and on and I could see the anxiety in my parents' faces. My mother would try to comfort my father and say, 'It's a child's ailment and the doctors will soon make her well.' At that time we were living in the police quarters in Byculla where the air was quite polluted; on one side was the Byculla railway station with coal puffing engines; there were no electric trains at that time, and all around us were mills with chimneys belching smoke.

My father realized what I needed most was clean fresh air. I remember being woken up early in the morning and taken in a victoria (a horse *gharry*) to Mahalakshmi, where we would stop along the sea front and I would take deep breaths to fill my lungs with the pure fresh air. My father made this into a fascinating game and I would enjoy every minute of it. I also loved the drive there and back on the quiet empty roads.

When my parents first met and fell in love, my father was a widower, he had lost his wife and two small children. His wife had been a Catholic. He knew my mother was also a Catholic, and although he belonged to the Church of England, he was not a staunch churchgoer. He knew the rules of the Catholic church in a mixed marriage. A document would have to be signed that any children from the marriage would be baptised as Catholics and that the marriage service would be in a Catholic church. He told my mother that there would be no problems as he was willing and quite agreeable to abide by these rules. I was seven years old when I made my First Holy Communion and as my father was a Protestant, I did not expect him to be present at the ceremony in the Catholic church. As we children came out of the church to greet our parents, my eyes fell on my father's face. He had come after all and looked at me with such love and pride that my little seven-year-old heart skipped a beat. After my sister and I were married and had left home, my father gave my mother a wonderful surprise. He told her he had gone to meet an English Catholic priest and had started taking instructions in the Catholic faith. It was a happy day for our whole family when the final baptism took place, and we then would attend church services together. In passing, I must mention that both my sister and I married Protestants who later became Roman Catholics.

 A lesson my father taught my sister and me was never to treat a promise lightly and that if we ever made a promise we must keep it. He never broke his promises to us and so we grew up with complete trust in him. Sometimes he would say, 'I can't promise, but I'll do my best', and it was consolation enough for us. He also taught us to have consideration and regard for neighbours; we were never allowed to play music or talk in a loud manner after ten at night or bang car doors when we returned home late from a dance or party.

 My father loved classical music and had a passion for opera. I also grew to love music and this gladdened my father's heart. So with good teachers, encouragement from my father, talent and hard work, I was able to achieve the highest diplomas of both the Trinity College and the Royal Academy. My mother and sister were not so keen, so whenever a celebrated violinist, pianist or an opera company visited Bombay, my father and I would go along together and have long discussions on the way back home on the merit of the performers; he made me laugh so much once when he told me that one of the singers sounded like she was cawing. We were all very fond of songs made famous by Bing Crosby, Frank Sinatra and, of course, Nat King Cole. My mother played the mandolin, an instrument rarely heard today, and our evenings were full of music and laughter.

My father was a quiet person but he could be witty and loved company. One day, he sat contentedly puffing away at his pipe while my mother, as usual, occupied herself with some sort of needlework. Watching her, my father said, 'Why don't you just sit back and relax, for a change?' Smiling at him, she said, 'All right, light me up a pipe then and we can both relax and enjoy a smoke together.' They were both very good at repartee, sometimes funny but never rude, and my sister and I thoroughly enjoyed being at home with them. There was always a deep and enveloping warmth between us and our parents.

One of my father's most prized possessions was a postcard from the Vatican in Rome. It was the Pope's jubilee year, 1933-1934, and the address on the card ended 'Bombay, India Britannica'. It was from the Holy Father, thanking him for being a kind and generous benefactor to the Mount Poinsur orphanage at Borivli. My father was generous and compassionate and besides giving a monthly donation, he would take my sister and me during our Divali and Christmas holidays to visit different institutions, our car loaded with sweets and baskets of fruits. We would mingle with the children and other residents and have a wonderful and happy time. Another favourite institution was the St. Joseph's Nursery and Foundling Home in Byculla where nuns looked after abandoned babies and older children. Whenever they had P.T. displays or an elocution contest, my sister and I would be asked to be judges. The children were well trained and my father would feel proud and honoured that his daughters had been asked to judge their performances.

I knew my father had a temper, he wouldn't tolerate us arguing with our mother or being disobedient to her. One day, while sitting at table over lunch, my sister, then seventeen, got into an argument with my father. She had a sharp and caustic tongue and thought she knew more than him. The argument had something to do with the scriptures which she had learnt for the Cambridge examinations which she passed with very high marks, even a distinction, so when this silly argument over the Gospel of St. John came up, she was rude and sarcastic. Suddenly he got up from his chair with his hand raised and walked towards her. My mother and I were shocked as he had never before struck either of us girls. When he came up to my sister he put his hand down and said, 'Watch that tongue of yours, my girl.' That night when she went to kiss him goodnight she said she was very sorry for the way she had behaved. He hugged her and said, 'Take the advice I gave you, it might make all the difference one day between happiness or despair for you.'

A few days after my eighteenth birthday, my father took me to the Police Headquarters to get a learner's driving license. He was keen that I should become a good and careful driver. He and the chauffeur took turns to teach me. After the three-months learning period I went back with my father to the Head Office for my driving test; I was terribly nervous but I passed. A few days later a funny incident happened. My sister and I were going to see a movie at the old Wellington picture house. We were late and my sister egged me on to drive faster. Queen's Road at 3.15 p.m. was quite empty of traffic so I really pressed down on the accelerator. Suddenly from behind us we heard the nonstop hooter of a motorcycle and knew at once it was a traffic cop; luckily he was a friend. He asked me what did I think I was doing and didn't I know I was breaking the speed limit? I smiled at him innocently and told him that we were already late for the show at Wellington. 'Follow me,' he said with a big grin and got us to the show on time. When we returned home we laughingly mentioned this to father. His rebuke was mild but I could see he was upset and I took care not to repeat it.

When I was studying for my final music examinations, a young man came into my life. I was only eighteen and the thought of marriage had not occurred to me; I naively thought we were just good friends. So when he proposed to me, I was terrified. I knew if I mentioned this to my father he would be bitterly disappointed as I had two more years left to reach my goal. The young man, however, was adamant and stood firm and since 'faint heart never won fair lady' he came to meet my father. After the usual greetings neither of them spoke. The young man was embarrassed and nervous and didn't know how to begin. After a long silence which my father did nothing to relieve, the young man seeing him contentedly pulling on his pipe, said, 'I see you enjoy smoking a pipe.' My father said, 'Yes, and what do you smoke?' My mother who was listening from the bedroom, came out and interrupted, 'This young man has not come to talk about pipes and cigarettes, he has come to talk about your daughter.' Everyone laughed and the atmosphere eased when my father realized that the young man was willing to wait till I finished my music examinations.

My wedding present from my parents was a beautiful Allison piano. The ceremony was performed in the quaint old St. Ann's Church in Mazagaon. My father was in full dress regalia with silver spurs on his shoes and two silver crowns on his mess jacket and looked ever so distinguished and handsome. I was so proud of him and as he led me down the aisle I felt it was the happiest day of my life. The reception was at the Police Club and it was a champagne affair with just family and a few dear friends. Fourteen months later, my father was delighted to be asked to be my baby's godfather, and on the day of his grandson's birth he opened a bank account in his and the baby's name.

My father had kept in touch with his mother until her death, and also with a favourite aunt called Sarah after whom I was named. After his mother's death his eldest sister carried on the correspondence. In 1942 this sister's son came out to India with his regiment; Japan had then entered the war and a large number of British troops were stationed in Bombay. Having my father's telephone number and address, he phoned to say he would like to visit him. He came but the visit was not repeated and my father guessed it was because of racial prejudice—my mother was Indian. She belonged to the East Indian community and was a cultured woman and a good artist.

When the Japanese had overrun Southeast Asia and there was a very real threat to India, Father, who had long retired, joined the Air Raid Patrol. He was now seventy but took his duties in the ARP very seriously. The moment an air raid alarm sounded, he would put on his tin hat, take his whistle and see that the roads were empty and everybody safely under cover. He was quite strict and allowed nobody to break the rules.

My father's last illness was long and painful but he was always cheerful and tried to encourage us. It was a serious heart case and so he could no longer enjoy his pipe or cigar and would long for me to come and sit near him and smoke a cigarette—just the smell of the tobacco would comfort him. It was so little that I could do for him, after all the years he had spent guiding and loving me.

He was always kind and generous and I knew I would miss him terribly. He died on 10 January 1950, just sixteen days before India became a republic. I cannot end this without mentioning a beautiful passage written by Simon Pereira, editor of the *Sunday Standard*, about my father, which I feel truly portrays him: 'Superintendent Jack Shaw retained to the last the warm heart and kind nature of a man who was human to the core, filled with the sympathy that wins confidence as well as love.'

Chapter Eleven

Mixed Signals
Shyamala Ramayya Raman

My father was a man whose psyche and personality were moulded in a pleasant childhood at a maternal uncle's home in a small village near Mayavaram in Tamil Nadu. He went to high school and college in Kumbakonam and later to Madras Christian College, growing with each experience. He acquired idiosyncrasies and matured as his work took him across India, finally mellowing in retirement. Within my father's story is mine, that of an unexpected daughter who was at once exposed to entrenched attitudes towards women and yet helped to blossom in ways that were unusual in her family.

Twenty-second January marks the anniversary of Appa's death. On that day, each year, I replay in my mind the memories of the visit to India I made specifically to say goodbye to him. I spent two weeks watching him wither away and yet he had the energy to talk about history, my life in the United States and his farewell to the world. On the day I was leaving Madras, 14 January 1986, he asked me to stay for a week longer, but I foolishly said that my academic schedule required my immediate return. His final goodbye was a very strong hug, unusual for a man who was most undemonstrative, with the blessing, 'May only good things happen in your life.' This memory replay serves each year, as a frame for reflecting on the ties that bound us.

My relationship to Appa was a caring yet difficult one. On reflection, with the wisdom of hindsight, I would say that though he was an unbending patriarch imbued with all the patriarchal values of his time, I still admire him more than any other male member of my family. I do not say that flippantly. I do have some unpleasant memories in my relationship with my father that I would like to erase, but ultimately what stands out is his legacy of learning and the steadfast values that he so cherished. Today when I am given a compliment, I attribute it to Appa's blessings.

Appa's name had a distinct Telugu sound to it which intrigued me. He explained that in the seventeenth century, his ancestor Swarna Sastry moved from the historic Vijayanagar area of Andhra to Semmangudi village in Tamil Nadu. Nine generations later, my grandfather, Sama Iyer, was a reasonably well-off landlord in Semmangudi, very conscious of making a name among the feudal 'eighteen-village' Vathimas who are a sub-sect of the Tamil Iyers, spread out in Tamil Nadu and Kerala. The families belonging to the eighteen villages near Thanjavur were known for their agricultural wealth, small families and frugality. Interestingly enough, this small community nurtured several eminent musicians. Vathima girls used to be married off around thirteen years of age—there was absolutely no question of educating them. Much of this has changed now.

Sama Iyer went on to become a municipal councillor, and though he had not received any formal education, he was convinced that the path to success for his sons, of whom my father was the eldest, was more likely to be through education than through agricultural landholding. He wanted to show the community that his sons were college-educated. He was the first Vathima to buy a Model T Ford in Kumbakonam. Appa was the first Vathima to receive a master's degree and enter the government services. Sama Iyer moved to Kumbakonam and established a household there so that his sons could attend the Town High School and later go to colleges in Madras. My father outshone his siblings, completing his masters' degree with a university rank and prizes. Though one of his brothers went on to become a famous writer under the pen name of 'Mowni' and the other took a law degree, both chose to manage their agricultural properties. Appa sat for the competitive examinations and joined the Indian Audit and Accounts Service in 1928. This was the typical route taken by most bright young South Indian men of that time, becoming willing bureaucrats in the service of the Empire, exactly as Lord Macaulay had wanted, through the spread of English education. It was a matter of prestige to enter these services and little did the entrants think of themselves as protagonists of the colonial agenda. These young men had to make major transitions from the villages in which they had grown up to cities like Bombay and Calcutta where they were posted in their probationary years. Unwittingly or as a matter of survival, a number of these bureaucrats became 'brown sahebs'. Today, when we look at this situation through the critical lens of postcolonial theory, we are appalled that the 'steel frame' and the derivative services were so highly valued.

Appa kept a diary for sixty years, 1926–1986. After he died, my brother asked if I wanted the collection as otherwise it was to be discarded. I did not ask for the entire set and decided to take the diaries for the years that each of us children were born (1931, 1933, 1936 and 1946) and for 1969, the year that I left India. I am grateful that I took these because they contain vignettes of his inner struggles, his great obsession with personal health, small professional triumphs and commentaries on history, art, culture, politics, family and friends.

I am the fourth and last child of my parents. My arrival into this world was an accident—a matter of embarrassment to my parents who had just celebrated the wedding of their first-born, Kamala, aged fourteen, during the summer of 1945. As I was growing up, I would often hear what a beautiful wedding it was, with four days of celebrations. Kamala had just finished high school at the Church Park Convent. No one ever gave thought to the fact that this child was being married. What mattered were the wedding festivities and the agricultural holdings of the groom's family. My brother-in-law was eighteen and had great potential according to the astrologers.

It was after Kamala's wedding that my mother found herself pregnant. It was entirely unintended. Appa was transferred to Ranchi as Comptroller of the state of Bihar, and my pregnant mother was left in Madras to run a household with my two siblings as well as the young married couple. It was a very difficult pregnancy, and my mother did not have proper prenatal care or any of the nurturing that is given to pregnant women. I was her fifth pregnancy and she had three surviving children. My cousin Kunju's husband, a physician, whom we all call Doctor, assisted the midwife when I was born prematurely at home. My father was at Ranchi. The entry in his diary for Friday, 11 January 1946 reads: 'Happy news. I get telegram from Father about the birth of a girl; let her live long and bring luck to me.'

He got to see me eighteen months later on his annual leave. My mother was much troubled with the responsibility of running a large household and taking care of a prematurely born, constantly wailing infant. Kamala often tells me that it was she who took care of me, provided the attentive care and love so essential in infancy, fondly feeding me curds and rice and dried lime pickles so that I soon gained weight and was as healthy as full-term babies. My parents were embarrassed by my arrival. Many friends and relatives kept questioning them, mistaking me to be the child of my sister and her husband, Jayaraman.

I do not remember any significant interaction with my father until my eighth birthday. We were then in Madras, living in a huge bungalow. By this time, I had been to three schools, in Ranchi, Trivandrum and now in Madras. Appa was inspired to arrange a beautiful birthday party for me. Invitations with green lettering on grey paper were printed by Krishnamurthy Mama, a favourite friend of Appa's, and Uncle Jal Batlivala was assigned to take pictures and show movies. A happy bunch of friends from my school were invited and the whole event was memorable. I still recall the happiness I felt at being the centre of attention. In my mind, this event began a bonding which had been so sorely neglected when I was born.

I also remember our holiday trips to hill stations—Ooty and Kodi—during the two years he was posted at Madras. Once Appa organized a concert by M. S. Subbalakshmi at our house to felicitate his distant cousin, the eminent musician Semmangudi Srinivasa Iyer. For me, aged eight, these were introductions to the life he loved. And I was also introduced to his temper. When he got upset, Mother told us children, 'Appa is unpleasant today.' He could get upset for the slightest reason: the sambhar having a tad less or more salt could be the trigger, or the newspaper not being delivered at 6 a.m. or by something at the office. Whatever it was, I learnt not to aggravate it by appearing in front of him. It became such a habit that before I even spoke to him, I measured his degree of 'unpleasantness' or 'pleasantness'.

To enable us to live on in Madras while he was sent on assignments, Appa built a house in Madras that he named 'Vijaya', his pride and joy. He swore that it would never be rented; my mother would stay back in the house with the three of us while father was transferred to other cities. In 1957, my sister Radha was married soon after her graduation; my brother's marriage took place in the following year, so now my father felt that my mother should move to Hyderabad where he was Accountant-General of Andhra Pradesh. It meant yet one more change of schools for me, but the brief period with Appa opened up a new phase of my relationship with him.

It was in Hyderabad that I again saw facets of Appa's tenderness, his sense of duty to his family and, of course, his temper. It was in Hyderabad that I learnt to love Indian history and acquired a taste for art, major influences in my early teens. I also got the intimations of how I was to be 'protected' till I was married. This meant that I was kept away from boys and any normal adolescent entertainment, such as parties, movies, and so on. I never could understand why my parents were so paranoid about guarding me. On the one hand I enjoyed our Friday evening outings to Abid Road, the walks along the Hussain Sagar Bund, the trips to Golconda Fort, Falaknuma Palace, the Salar Jung Museum, Nagarjunakonda; the visits of scholars and painters to our home. On the other hand I could never understand the strict rules imposed on me. I would write over and over again in my diary—'I wish my parents were not so strict.' All the while, Appa was consciously kindling my interest in a number of areas, awakening me to the liberal arts, current events and the world of economics and finance. When I look back now, I may have missed going to the movies or parties, but I did have a different kind of a good time, taking in trips to historical sites and meeting scholars and visitors.

My mother and I returned to Madras in the middle of 1959 and I found myself back in Vidyodaya, my old school, to complete the last one and a half years of matriculation. I went on to enjoy undergraduate life at Ethiraj College, participating in both curricular and extracurricular activities to the hilt, subject to the constraint of the extremely rigid time and 'protection' strictures. Appa retired in 1963 and returned to his favourite 'Vijaya'. The next few years until my marriage in 1969, cemented my relationship with Appa and at the same time kept me wondering why he had the deep-seated need to protect me. It was as though they had to make sure they raised a daughter who was to be offered as a virgin to whomever they chose for a husband. Yet there was absolutely no chance that something 'untowards' would happen. I went to a girls' college and even did my postgraduate degree at a women's college. When my parents visited their friends, either I had to go with them or they would make arrangements for *kaval* (vigil) by the maidservant.

I was interested in sports and wanted to join the T. Nagar Ladies Club to learn tennis but Appa would not allow this as he was worried about the coach and the ball boys. Coming home to my diary I wrote, 'Why are my parents so afraid—why cannot they trust me?' If I spoke at debates, the college had to make sure there was an escort for me. If I was the lone passenger in the car, the maidservant was always there. My friends at school and college would find all this highly amusing. Why, I could not even sit on the same sofa with my brother-in-law!

What is paradoxical is that Appa so intently watched over my intellectual growth at this stage. He was very particular that I should be an all-rounder, and to this end encouraged me to participate in inter-collegiate debates, read Dale Carnegie and even try my hand at painting. Now that he had retired, he zealously went to the libraries and brought back books on economics; I was not allowed to go to the Connemara or the university library so I devised a way of getting the books through the law clerk of one of my friends. I guess I was very resilient, for even as I felt depressed and sad under these stifling rules, I managed to create a life of some cheer. I was given driving lessons by Appa on the Marina, with severe reprimands for trifling errors. I was coached in public speaking in the upstairs hall of 'Vijaya'. I would follow all of Appa's wishes because I was terrifed of his displeasure. My poor mother bore the brunt, though, because I would constantly whine to her. She would call me a *pudungu* ('whiner'). Then she would go on about how I was a liability and a burden in their old age. Such put-downs would sear my psyche. I never knew where I stood except that I had to fulfil the expectations of my parents and teachers. It was as though I was constantly listening to mixed signals.

In 1965 when I graduated in economics, most of my friends were getting married. My mother wanted to start the process of looking for a match for me, but my father insisted that I join the master's course in economics—at a women's institution, of course. I could not go to the university or to the coeducational Madras Christian College and certainly not out of Madras, so we settled for Stella Maris College. My father was very interested in my curriculum and would take an hour each night to talk about Keynes and other economists. I found the academic work extremely rigorous and demanding and would vent my frustration on my mother. Around the second year of my course, the matrimonial search began. It was rather demeaning to be 'viewed' by prospective young men. It made me irritable; had I been a man, I would not have had to go through this process. I remember Appa and my mother discussing how difficult it was to find a match for me. My dormant feminist conscience began to rumble but not loud enough because I would suffer these indignities lest I upset my father and make him 'unpleasant'. This went on for two years until my marriage was arranged. Of course, in my parents' books, they were being very modern as they would inform me about the prospective match, his qualifications and his family. I have all the letters that went back and forth between my father and father-in-law before my wedding. Both of them considered themselves progressive as they had educated their respective daughters to high levels, but what came through from my father's letters was both pride in his daughter's accomplishments and the willingness to accommodate the schedules of my husband's family for the wedding. While my father-in-law shocked my father by not accepting any dowry, I could detect in his letters that he was looking for the bride to fulfil all the needs of his son. There was never a consideration that marriage was a union for the flowering of each partner for the good of the newly created joint unit. It was unilaterally expected that no matter how well the girl was educationally endowed, she was there for the convenience of the ultimate decision-maker—the man. It takes about twenty years into such marriages to realize the unequal nature of the relationship and all the heartache that it entails.

Looking back today I am grateful for the lecture, harsh though it was, that I received from my father on the day after my marriage. My father sat me down and told me that marriage was an imperfect institution at best. Therefore, I should not be totally trusting of my spouse; I should always maintain separate financial accounts and develop interests of my own. I have done so and these serve as wonderful anchors during some very rough times. It is strange that he said this to me because he certainly did not allow my mother to have her own finances or for that matter to develop her interests such as playing bridge. On the contrary, he stifled many of her interests and never allowed her to reach her potential. That is still the norm with many of the men in my family.

Appa blew hot and cold. At one moment, he would be most considerate of me and my future and at the next he would summon me upstairs to his room and show me the accounts of the wedding. I would nag my mother and moan that my biggest misfortune was being born, I had never asked to be born. Appa would go for days without speaking to me, hurting me very much. Even on the day I was leaving for the United States, he did not speak to me because he was annoyed with me. His entry in his diary dated Wednesday, 26 November 1969 reads:

Shyamala's Departure for America.
I reduce my tension towards her and become normal. My emotions start surging when the departure time nears. I try to control it by having a long chat with Radha, Chellam [son-in-law] on our future plans. Plane takes off at 11 p. m. I pat Shyam and ask her to be of good cheer. She was with us for 23 years and 11 months.

The next few entries in the diary are very poignant, showing the unarticulated affection of a father for a daughter. If only he had been more demonstrative, I would not have walked around with a complex, forever trying to please him and all the while being so afraid of him too. This has had quite an impact on my self-esteem. I have never been able to know who I am and what my capabilities are, and am always surprised when people compliment me.

A few extracts from his 1969 diary immediately after my departure.

27 November
I break down completely after return from station at 1.30 p.m. Bursts of terrific weeping and gusts of uncontrollable emotion sweep me every half hour. My anguish and grief is extreme. Wife is aghast. Her grief though deep, she feels, pales before mine. She has her good womanly instincts. She tries to console me. Am I selfish. Shyam and Raman's beautiful life starting... We want them [daughters] to be with us all of life.

28 November
Shyam's first day in America... she was part of this house and in the morning when I don't see her, I burst into tears. I have become weak! Age! Shyamala of course is a priceless girl; one in a lakh.

30 November
Fourth Day of Shyamala's Departure
Today I feel normal: except in the evening a little emotion. I am slowly getting over the anguish of Shyam's departure. We now want her to settle down happily . . .

Appa never intended that anyone should snoop into his precious diaries, which was one reason that my brother had said that discarding them would be the most appropriate thing to do.

However, I have taken the liberty to quote from them to show the Victorian struggle our fathers had in blending a concoction of colonialist, modern and feudalistic sensibilities when they tried to raise us in ways that they themselves had never known. So naturally they made mistakes along the way. These stories must be told so that there is a record of not only their lives but how they raised and moulded us, their daughters, with none of the paraphernalia of modern psychology or Benjamin Spock.

On a cold December morning in Providence, Rhode Island, soon after my arrival in the United States, I received a letter from Appa. I was completely bowled over when I opened it. He wrote:

> Immediately after your departure for a number of days both of us were very much upset emotionally. Then I wrote a few lines in great anguish to relieve my feelings.
>
> To Shyam on Her Departure
> Lo! Like a bird on wings thou flew away
> to the West from thine parental nest
> . . . .
> Thy parents see you far off
> In a cozy nest under beloved Ram's protecting wings
> Ah, what happiness, what cheer admits their tears.
> S. Ramayya 13.12.69

Even to this day, when I read these lines I am overcome with emotion. While Appa was fond of all his children, he never demonstrated his feelings. Always conscious of his duty as a father, he had been a tremendous source of moral and financial support when we went through crises in our lives. I do feel fortunate even though my father was such a tantalizing mix of strictness and authority and parental love that I never knew what to expect. Appa's letters to me after I went to the United States were always full of advice, family happenings and an occasional statement of missing me. I particularly remember one letter in which he said, 'The jasmine creepers along the front verandah send whiffs of fragrance and ask where is the girl who would so lovingly pick the flowers? And I tell them that she has flown away to the West.'

My visits back to India during his lifetime were very pleasant. There were none of the agonies of the past—there was no need to 'protect' me now that the task had been passed to Raman. Appa would shower me with additions to my library and wardrobe. He was also particular about my visiting our relatives in Thanjavur district, which I did in 1978. That was the last time I saw my writer uncle, Mowni.

By today's standards of psychotherapy, I may have had many scars as a child but these were nothing compared to the traumas one hears about today—incest and physical abuse. Appa must have thought that his parenting skills had improved with practice and that he was more lenient with me than towards my siblings. According to my siblings and their offspring, I was the apple of my parents' eyes. But deep layers of entrenched attitudes towards women made him act in very harsh ways. I learnt to be resilient and reflective because of these experiences and at the same time appreciated the precious gift of the life of the mind with which he so generously endowed me. I regard this gift of Appa's as the most valuable and imperishable asset that I received from him; this is what I meant when I wrote earlier that it was a caring but difficult relationship.

Appa lived and breathed history. From the days in Allahabad and later in Hyderabad and finally in Madras, he was hosting salons as it were, but we never gave it that fancy name. I was a beneficiary of this atmosphere more than any of my siblings and loved every minute of it. He would sit down in the special history artifacts room at 'Vijaya' and share with others his own interests. On Sundays he looked forward to a leisurely visit and a history-filled chat with eminent archaeologists, numismatists and art historians. His passion for analysing the Satavahana coins in his collection led to several articles in the *Journal of the Numismatic Society of India*. His interest in archaeology, numismatics and painting enabled him to spend his retirement years in endless research and writing. I certainly think this sustained pursuit of knowledge in one lifetime was a phenomenal leap from where he had begun.

Appa had an uncanny vision of what would happen in the future built on his wonderful historical sense of the past. In his contributions to *Commerce*, a business periodical, he said that the days of the generalist administrator and the bureaucratic structure as it then existed, were numbered. That was quite prophetic. He wrote about the wastefulness of large dams and their impact on agriculture. He was very savvy in the selection of his stock portfolio. Everything he told me about India's economy, the changing profile of the city of Madras, the shifting paradigms in education, were all on the mark. Similarly, his acceptance of all religions and castes had a major impact on me. Even as he was suffering from the excruciating pain of his illness during his last days, he would quote verses from the Book of Job. Today, when I speak on multiculturalism in the United States, I often pay tribute to Appa and tell the audience that they will be richer for learning about other cultures and should not look at the prospect with fear or assumed superiority. Appa also instilled in me a respect for integrity and steadfastness in all my undertakings, all the more to be appreciated in this time of disappearing values.

The then President of India, R. Venkataraman, was a student of my father's in the twenties, when my father had taught for a brief while. He had always kept in touch with our family and had even visited my father as late as in 1985. Appa had a way of forging relationships that lasted a lifetime, and as I grow older, I find the same thing happening in my life. I was touched when the President replied to a letter from me:

'Thank you for your letter of December, 18, 1990, which brought very pleasant recollections of your late father, Sri. S. Ramayya. He belonged to the increasingly rare category of *karma yogis* among civil servants.'

Appa is now part of the history that he so loved. When I search my mind for the highlights of his story as I saw it, I thank him each night for endowing me with the foundation to be a strong woman sustained by the joys of learning. Having had the strength to face the vicissitudes of my life during the last quarter century, I feel very privileged.

Chapter Twelve

Pressing the Wrong Nerve

By Usha Kumar

Recollecting memories of my father, who lived for almost eighty years, revives many feelings and associations. Not all of these form a cohesive picture of a man who exerted a tremendous influence on my life. Yet there are a few strands which emerge with regularity and weave disparate experiences of him into a pattern, as if it were his life-script. One of these strands is his controlled struggle to balance his dark inner feelings and apprehensions with moral correctness and fair play. Another is his intense desire to be recognized, applauded and loved. And all these within the overall framework to better himself. These driving forces became fairly transparent vulnerabilities in old age, when both his defences and intellect had weakened. It saddened me to see that the hero of our childhood had feet of clay. When I was not overwrought with my own personal concerns, I tried hard in those years to help him maintain control, at least, over himself and to accord him the respect which he sorely needed for his well-being.

In the last decade of his life, especially after the death of my mother, he was fraught with the fear of being left alone to fend for himself. None of his three children could live with him permanently. Nor did he make it easy for those who tried. He clearly needed caring and warmth but invariably elicited hurt and distance. 'He somehow presses the wrong nerve,' explained my sister. His children, now in the sixth decade of their lives, were progressively perceived as objects who could deliver the 'services' he desired but were somewhat devalued as individuals.

In the last few years, day after day, he sat silhouetted against the wall, working stoically at his desk—he published three books in these years—one of which ironically was titled *How to Grow Old Gracefully* or something to that effect, a sad picture of loneliness and isolation. His physical disabilities, poor vision and later Parkinson's disease restricted his movements. He made his life very structured. What had passed off as a disciplined life earlier and had proved functional became rigid and progressively dysfunctional. It prevented him from getting what he most desired and needed—companionship. For instance, he left me absolutely stunned when I went to visit him early one morning after I had come in from Kanpur to Delhi on some work. I reached home after a 45-minute drive through traffic, and he said, 'I am very busy in the morning. I have no time now,' and then quickly disappeared into his bedroom, signalling that the meeting was over. And, yet, though he wanted people on his terms and at his convenience, there were times when he responded to feelings. When I lost my dog, he knew I would be very upset, and as he could not come himself, ordered my sister to visit me immediately.

He was not generous with people. He appeared somewhat manipulative when he needed help. There were problems of give and take. He could understand how these problems erupted, but found himself powerless to control the inner anger at the turn of events. He could only find one reason for his inability to change, namely, his early childhood deprivation. There was a modicum of truth in what he observed. The scars of early life not visible before in the ineffective strategies frequently practised in a joint family to maintain superficial relationships had started to appear during the last phase of his life.

My pitaji, Sardari Lal Kumar, was born in 1903 in Hafizabad, a small village in undivided Punjab. His father was headmaster of the village primary school. Sardari Lal was the youngest of seven children and, not unusual in joint families, his closest playmate was a nephew of the same age. Times were hard and his father's death in the influenza epidemic of 1918 left the family totally dependent on his oldest brother.

Pitaji was academically brilliant, consistently topping the list of state candidates and went through school and college entirely on scholarships. He rounded off his record coming first in his batch and having his name engraved on the roll call of honour of the prestigious Thompson Engineering College, Roorkee, where he was able to complete the five year degree with a loan from the Sir Ganga Ram Trust. These five years were probably his happiest. He talked often about his participation in a variety of activities—camp-outs, photography, bridge, tennis, chess and whatever else was available. He also acquired a reputation as a sort of unofficial tutor-in-residence helping other students when they had difficulties. He once recounted to us how just before the final examination, when competition among students was keenest as jobs depended on their position in class, he lent his notes to his nearest rival.

Shortly after, Pitaji was inducted as an officer in the Indian Railways, then very much a preserve of the British. In the eyes of the world he had arrived. A classmate, who had kept track of him, approached him with a proposal of marriage with his sister. She was nineteen and came from a progressive, affluent landowning family. My maternal grandfather was a successful criminal lawyer. My father, who was twenty-three, married the next year. There is a charming story of how before the wedding, he tailed the tonga which took the daughter of the house for an outing to enjoy evenings outside the city. The elders of the family actually talked of it as a coincidence, but my aunts who believed otherwise teased my mother.

There was considerable disparity between my parents' educational levels. Mother had studied only up to the Eighth Standard, she could neither speak nor write English, a fact my father set out to rectify after the marriage. An Englishwoman was hired to teach her conversational English. She was taken repeatedly to the English refreshment rooms at railway stations to learn table manners and English etiquette. He wanted my mother to be presentable among his English colleagues. I am sure Mother found these exercises an imposition. She was not academically inclined, but learn she did, although she always hesitated to speak English in front of her children.

The marriage started on an unhappy note for my mother. Being indebted to his brothers for his upbringing, Pitaji could not refuse to take on the responsibility of providing for their mother, widowed sister and nephew. Mother accepted this. But when her trousseau was hijacked for the niece's wedding which was timed conveniently to follow hers, mother's joyful anticipation of wearing the finery she had brought with her, turned to unhappiness. She never forgave Pitaji for not standing up to his brothers, and her contempt for his family never let up.

Burdened with the family's demands Pitaji had, in the early years, to struggle to meet his financial commitments. Three children were born within five years. Mother's family held him in high regard and there was ample support from them.

My mother felt the intellectual domination of my father, but being a practical woman she was not overawed by his theoretical notions. The kind of companionship that my father and my mother developed over a long fifty years could not have been without the expected conflicts between married couples. But where the children were concerned there was a joint front. Pitaji always went along with any disciplining meted out to us by her.

My mother was socially very charming and she learnt to compensate for Pitaji's awkwardness with people. It was not that he was an introvert, but more that he did not demonstrate warmth or affection. He must have fitted the job of a bureaucrat perfectly. He could play the role impersonally without being attuned to the feelings of others. My mother made up for these deficiencies well, often whispering the name and identity of an approaching figure to Pitaji, who had obviously failed to recognize the individual. My mother mediated between Pitaji and the children, cushioning the impact of Pitaji's less than tactful observations.

Pitaji shared a lot with my mother, especially his dilemmas at the workplace. It was a very talk-oriented relationship. My mother would also read magazines written in Punjabi to him. My father was fairly enamoured of communist ideology and at one time debated buying land to build a house in an ideologically run commune. I am convinced my mother dissuaded him from following this fantasy. This was a passing phase in Pitaji's life, when he also experimented with diet fads, astrology and other esoteric stuff.

How devoted my parents were to each other became more than apparent when my mother became afflicted with terminal cancer. He bravely bore the wrath which patients suffering from chronic illness are prone to express to their healthy caretakers. My mother did not spare him but she also felt that she was very fortunate to have been provided the care which Pitaji gave her despite his own old age. He read books on this subject, tried various treatments, started her on vitamins, homeopathy, indigenous cures and kept up the struggle despite the losing battle: He did not spare himself. And my mother's dying concern was for Pitaji, who she knew would be lost without her.

I do not think Pitaji looked at any other woman during his lifetime. But I do recall my mother's insecurity when we met a distant relative in Ooty during a holiday trip. The wife of this gentleman was a very versatile housekeeper and a gardener. Furthermore, she could engage in intelligent conversation. I remember my father praising her (possibly he overdid it) and telling my mother to learn how to bake wheat bread at home from her. My mother bristled all the time, berated herself as not very educated and made Pitaji suffer through her noncooperation during the remainder of our stay. Pitaji's clarifications and apologies were of no avail.

Pitaji did keep a tight control over money even though he handed his whole salary to my mother. He also gave her whatever he saved from his travelling allowance, a sum not accountable to him. Despite the exercise of writing *hisab* for every *paisa* spent daily (which was open for 'audit' by my father any time) she did collect money of her own. Though Pitaji had financial constraints in his early married life, we children never felt deprived. Our home was abundantly stocked with fruits, nuts and snacks. And there was hospitality for all those who visited us. However, after Mother's death he did not always balance his give-and-take exercise. Maybe he had started to judge people's affection by what they brought with them when they came home (an error also made by many young people, I think). He would frequently tick me off for what I had brought, suggesting something quite different as his preference. He was becoming hard to please. I am not sure he really did not like the fuss we sometimes made over his birthday. But frequently he failed to act graciously during such times. It was sad to see a person who was oversensitive to any sign of rejection, fail to accept goodwill and love when these came his way.

My childhood memories of Pitaji are very happy ones. Gifts and toys and chocolate were balanced by books he brought for us. I learnt to read even before admission to school. We even went through a phase of celebrating Christmas with all the accompanying rituals of lights, crackers, caps and stockings filled with gifts, leaving us very happy memories.

School was a serious business with Pitaji, but he also emphasized games. He was a born teacher, and as we grew he took special delight in helping us with our studies. A class in general knowledge meant catching up with the morning's news, which he dictated to us, and my sister and I read this out in class much to our teacher's approval. Examinations meant hours in the evenings with Pitaji. Frequently Mother had to remind him not to overwork us. It was through his tutoring that I imbibed a love of numbers and understood their inherent beauty; this stood me in very good stead later in life when I had to master statistics.

A certain discipline and decorum was expected in the house. Everybody had to be dressed and ready for breakfast every morning. Our seats round the table were fixed. Here the family discussed activities planned by each of us. It was a fairly democratic forum and we could push things through if we had prepared our brief well. All meals were taken together even if it meant waiting up for Pitaji. It was an enjoyable ritual, though occasionally we were reprimanded for the day's transgressions. It was at the table that we got our lessons in nutrition, one of Pitaji's favourite interests. The virtues of proteins, vitamins, exercise were extolled ad nauseum. When I announced at breakfast one day my resolve to give up eating meat, Pitaji did not question it. His only comment was, 'Do see that you continue to get enough proteins.' It was as simple as that. We, as a family, still feel guilty if we do not eat right.

Travel, which was free for us, was another area of interest. He took us on long train trips to remote corners of undivided India. He then made us write about our experiences. We trudged through museums, zoos and historical sites. He did not tire. But we did. Pitaji, a keen photographer, kept chronological albums. Was he making up for what he had missed in his childhood, I wonder? I look back on those years with very warm feelings.

When Pitaji was transferred every three years, all of us except our brother moved with him. Our brother was admitted to a boarding school when he was five, much against Mother's wishes. Possibly it had an adverse affect and created much tension in the father-son relationship, particularly towards the end when the balance of power had changed in my brother's favour.

I started to sense a change in Pitaji when we moved from Lahore to Delhi during the partition of the country. These were very troubled times for the family. Many relatives could not be traced as they were stranded across the border. Pitaji was inundated with work. Day and night he was on the job, seeing to the administration of his division and to the safety of arriving and departing refugees. Our education was put on hold, so to say. If we had wanted to stay at home after high school my father would not have been unhappy.

I did manage to persuade Pitaji to send me to a college in

Lucknow where I completed my undergraduate studies. This was my first time away from home. This separation aroused considerable anxiety. My fear was that if I talked about my homesickness Pitaji's easy solution would be to bring me back home. We corresponded fairly regularly during these years and he displayed concern for my health and general welfare. This was the start of a different phase in my relationship with my father, changing my perceptions of him. I was in my late teens/early twenties and he in his mid-forties. We each must have been going through our own identity crisis and let our inner concerns dovetail with our outer ones—thus enmeshing and distorting perceptions of each other. We were both concerned about our futures. Pitaji's concern was totally invested in his career. He was an ambitious man. There was talk about colleagues, promotions and who was getting what posting. Maybe he was not getting his just dues. He had not suffered any setback so far and he was considered a very able officer. But he was not satisfied with a posting which took him away from Delhi to Lucknow, and he felt sidelined.

The fact that both my sisters and I had grown up and become adults was reflected in Pitaji's anxiety to see us married and settled. Since my sister's marriage was delayed for inexplicable reasons, I got a reprieve to study further. It was not in Pitaji's plan to send me beyond the undergraduate level. But he thought of graduate studies only as a stop-gap arrangement till my sister was married and he had found a suitable alliance for me. His early upbringing where people played appropriate roles exerted itself to mask his later liberal experiences. He appeared conservative in that he only wanted to fulfil his responsibilities. However, he was very reassuring in his resolve that he would not contract an arrangement without my consent.

At this time I also started making comparisons with friends and their experiences with parents. I was exposed to many different types of peers in the hostel. Fathers of friends seemed warm and demonstrative in their affection. By comparison, Pitaji was distant. Even his letters were signed with his name underneath in block letters! This was the time the aura around my father started to fade. I was not entirely astonished when in the course of a psychological projective test my response to the idea of father was a scarecrow. Despite these growing critical perceptions, I could not readily distance myself from him. I never did all through my life. During this phase I was emotionally bound and dependent upon him for acceptance and for a confirmation of my identity.

Subtle, covert and sometimes fairly contradictory messages were communicated in the tug-of-war of wills in the next few years of my relationship with Pitaji. Both parents were deeply concerned that I marry and settle down. They openly stated that they would support my choice if I was interested in someone. Yet they got very worried when I had an evening out with my brother and his friend at the club. I was told clearly that this was not permitted any more. Even a glass of cider was frowned upon. Such behaviour would make it increasingly difficult for them to find the right match! Gradually, restrictions and curbs increased. The last straw was the 'order' to quit my job and come back home. I had started to teach in my old college as soon as I had finished my master's degree and I was supporting myself financially and living on the college campus. This independence was perceived as unacceptable in our community for a young unmarried woman. No option was given. I had to comply. I lost my tenure and the prospect of financial aid from the college to study abroad.

I resolved to move away from this repressive atmosphere. I applied for a scholarship to go to the USA for studies and was awarded a grant. This was not in the scheme of things planned by Pitaji. A pall of gloom descended on him. He had thought that his noncooperation in providing finances would prevent me from going away. The grant was a comprehensive one and I did not need additional funds. All I needed was some emotional support. This he withheld. If I decided to go, he said, I had to go it alone and did so for the medical examination and other travel preparations which I managed on a modest budget. Only at the very last moment did my parents decide to accompany me to Bombay from where I had to sail. Something snapped in me at this time. I rarely, if ever, asked Pitaji for monetary help in later years.

My father had been retired for many years before I left for the USA. His retirement brought in a long period of uncertainty and financial worries. He had no house, in a way no place to go to. He stayed on in the railway guesthouse till his appointment as Principal of the Thapar Engineering College in Patiala came through. Settling children did not settle Pitaji, and he left Patiala before his term was up, moving to Delhi to construct a house.

Finally, my parents had a home of their own, and Pitaji found his moorings again. He tended a beautiful garden and many people consulted him as a homeopath. People praised him for his miraculous cures. He always treated people without any fees. He enjoyed closeness with people by sharing private and personal details of their symptoms elicited during diagnostic sessions. And dispensing medicine assured some kind of a sustained people contact but his meticulous study of patients gradually started to wane even though he carried on with his practice.

Returning after six years I was saddened to see the changes at home. Pitaji had aged considerably during this period and had slowed down both mentally and physically. My parents were living more frugally than was necessary or warranted by their financial resources. Their life-style was austere now.

I had returned with a doctorate in psychology, and shortly after I was appointed to a teaching post at IIT, Kanpur. I think it was the sort of job Pitaji had always dreamed of for himself as he had wanted to return to Roorkee as a professor. The question of marriage was dropped entirely, perhaps Pitaji felt that I was now quite capable of taking charge of my life. Though he was pleased that I had a post at IIT, I began to sense an odd ambivalence in Pitaji's reaction to my career. He seemed to see saw between pride at my achievements and a sort of unconscious envy which manifested itself in strange ways. He would often belittle me and sometimes even totally ignore my specialized skills. This was something at a deeper level than the general envy an older generation can feel sometimes at the vitality of and opportunities open to younger people, as compared to their own failing powers. He expressed a desire to go abroad himself soon after my return. The homeopathic association had recognized his contribution to the field in the two books he had written by conferring the title of Doctor on him. He informed me that he would not reply to my letters if I failed to append Dr. to his name. I was uncomfortable with the confused feelings evoked in me—pity and puzzlement. Was he still competing with me, his own child?

It is difficult to nurture hurt when you see a parent grow old and frail. I very consciously decided to do all I could not to make him unhappy. I had a full time job, but his welfare was very important for me and he must have realized this. When he became uncomfortable with his caretakers, he would send for me to share his pain. I wished he would change, and yet I was aware that he could not change his autocratic rigid ways. He wanted someone to wait upon him. Any delay brought on feelings of neglect and aroused his ire. He was charming, however, with visitors and relatives. But he could switch off very easily with his immediate family.

I am not sure what prompted the query from him as he had never before consulted me about his financial matters. He wanted me to advise him regarding his will. My suggestion was that this last act should come from his heart and not his head. Later, I was not sure if he was testing me. He could well have asked this question to my two siblings. I think his sense of fairplay outweighed all other considerations, especially the anger and disappointment he certainly suffered at the hands of his children.

Pitaji's end came suddenly. He was not sick. He was just tired. His earlier assertion that he wanted to live up to a hundred possibly did not matter any more. He was gradually pulling up his stakes, dissolving his assets. He was meditating longer and not interacting with others around him happily. He even agreed to leave Delhi to spend time with me in Hyderabad—something he would never have considered earlier. Despite the growing inevitability of losing an aged parent, his death came as a shock. I had thought he would live on forever. For me, an era came to end with his passing away.

I will always remain curious about what Pitaji thought of his family. His innumerable diaries maintained over half-a-century, possibly contained that information. There was very little inclination to read them now. I did not need his approval as I had several decades ago. To rake up the past seemed irrelevant. It was best to respect his privacy after his death as we did during his life. None of us read those diaries.

More now, than when he was alive, I am conscious of traits and habits in myself that are similar to Pitaji's. They are a part of me, whether I like it or not. I wonder if I have also absorbed the same drive for self-improvement and growth which he displayed all through his life.

List of Editors and Contributors

EDITORS

Priti T. Desai (born 1934) obtained her MA in economics from the University of Bombay. She taught briefly at Miranda House, Delhi, and then worked as a Woman-Friday in various spheres.

Neela D'Souza (born 1933) graduated with history honours from the University of Madras and received her MA in journalism from Syracuse University. She has taught history and written children's books, articles and 'middles' for newspapers.

Sonal Shukla (born 1941) studied literature, aesthetics and comparative education. She has worked with the Gandhian Institutes of Education and is the coordinator of Vacha, a women's resource centre in Bombay. She has made a film on women freedom fighters: *'Bheetar Bahe Mukti Dhara'* and contributes regularly to Gujarati newspapers.

CONTRIBUTORS

Mannu Bhandari (born 1931) spent her childhood in Ajmer. She received her MA from Benares Hindu University. Many of her short stories and novels have been translated into regional languages and English and have also been adapted for films and television.

Rinki Bhattacharya (born 1942) lived in Calcutta as a small child and then moved to Bombay with her family. She graduated from the University of Bombay and is an active feminist, columnist, writer and has also made documentaries and short films.

Bindu T. Desai (born 1948) is a neurologist who has lived in the USA for over two decades. She is a human rights activist and writes for Indian newspapers.

Usha Kumar (born 1932) graduated from Isabella Thoburn College, Lucknow, and obtained a PHD in clinical psychology from Ohio State University. She was professor of psychology, IIT Kanpur. Currently she is a consultant in the area of human resource development and lives in Hyderabad.

Sarah Major (born 1911) has lived all her life in Bombay. She is a homemaker and has taken a special interest in civic issues.

Iqbal Monani (born 1935) is a poet. She graduated with English honours and took a degree in law from the University of Bombay. Prior to her marriage, she was assistant editor, PEN (India).

Jane Pillai (born 1938) was born and educated in England. She graduated from the Royal College of Art, London, and taught in England and in India. A homemaker and a mother, she has lived in many parts of India and now resides in Trivandrum.

Shyamala Ramayya Raman (born 1946) grew up in Hyderabad and in Madras where she received her MA and moved to the USA after marriage. She has a PHD in economics and teaches at Saint Joseph College in West Hartford, Connecticut.

Rekha Rao (born 1947) studied painting under her artist father, K. K. Hebbar. She has held solo exhibitions since 1971, and participated in group shows since 1978 in India and abroad. Her paintings are in the National Gallery of Modern Art and at the Lalit Kala Academy.